Other Books by Ewen Southby-T[illegible]ylour

Militar[illegible]

[illegible]

Reasons in Writing: A [illegible] War

Amphibious Assault [illegible] for San Carlos

Blondie: A Life of Lieute[illegible]-Colonel HG Hasler, DSO., OBE

The Next Moon: A Special Operations Executive Agent in France

HMS Fearless: The Mighty Lion

3 Commando Brigade, Helmand

Commando Assault, Helmand

Nothing Impossible: A Portrait of The Royal Marines 1664 - 2010 (Editor)

Exocet Falklands: The Untold Story of Special Forces Operations

Paid to Predict: Duplicity, Deceit and Dishonesty among 'Allies'

Fiction

Skeletons for Sadness: A Story of Espionage, Love and War in the Falklands

Death's Sting: Duplicity and Deceit in the Balkans

Reference

Jane's Amphibious Warfare Capabilities (Editor)

Jane's Amphibious and Special Forces (Editor)

Jane's Special Forces Equipment Recognition Guide (Editor)

A Life in Letters

plus a selection of, very many, essays

Ewen Southby-Tailyour

First published in paperback by
Michael Terence Publishing in 2024
www.mtp.agency

ISBN 9781800947153

Michael Terence
Publishing

Introduction

I do not want anyone to be under any illusion: this is, purely and simply, a book for the Christmas stocking then the downstairs loo!

A Life in Letters is a collection of letters (plus a few essays at the end) written over the years to a number of unsuspecting recipients who would, most probably, have preferred never to have heard from me. That some of the following letters did make it on to the printed page surprised me each time I opened the morning paper or monthly magazine. Equally, I was very occasionally surprised that a letter on some relevant topic about which I happened to know a little did not make it into the 'public domain'.

Yet it would be very wrong of me if I did not admit that I never expected any offering to have been accepted while, in a number of cases, the moment I pressed 'send' or stuffed the envelope into the village letter box I wished I hadn't! Paradoxically of course, there are a few that I was sad did not see the light of day.

Many of these letters are frivolous, some are just plain silly, many are of no consequence, some I am embarrassed to have written and a fair few composed simply to let off steam but most were compiled in the hope that they might, at the very least, have highlighted a contemporary event or, perhaps, appealed to a reader's sense of the ridiculous. Some might even bring a wry smile to the breakfast table; they did to mine while I was typing them. A few are seriously serious and, indeed, historically thought-provoking: occasionally in support of an 'underdog' who has been poorly treated by 'the system'. They are not in chronological order but appear in the order in which they are stored in my computer, although I have tried to put those covering the same subject together. Often I have added a comment where an explanation clarifies the reason behind the letter. At the end I have added a few personal letters and reports that might, possibly, be of passing curiosity.

Rather obviously, as is the nature of letters to newspapers, many of these letters and essays are self-opinionated. Such letters usually are and, noticeably, written to offer an opposing point of view while others are written to establish a discussion. If they were not self-opinionated there would not be much point in sending them!

And why have I done this when, at my age, I should be relaxing by the log fire with a glass of whisky in one hand while the other hand strokes the ears of one of the three golden retrievers curled up at my feet?

The other evening, at supper, a friend complained about the number of times he was forced to see my name beneath yet another 'letter to the editor'. I told him he was lucky that he did not have to read the many that did not make it into print. "On the contrary," he said, "they might be more interesting."

So, interesting or not, here are most of them; published and unpublished.

Ewen Southby-Tailyour
South Devon, January 2024

Contents

The Daily Telegraph

General Topics

16th July 2022

On Thursday last my daughter flew to Bristol from Toulouse via Amsterdam. The pilot was a serious-sounding Frenchman but also one with the ability, through humour, to make sure that all announcements from the cockpit and the cabin crew were actually listened to. Part of one of his mid-flight broadcasts was, "We are flying at 37,000 feet - that is a very large number of shoes."

...

17th June 2021

[Allison Pearson - married to a half-first-cousin of mine - was arguing that, after lockdown, the country should revert to normal without any delay.]

I (and absolutely everyone I know) wholeheartedly endorse every word Allison Pearson wrote in yesterday's paper. Good, old-fashioned (but out of fashion) common sense that really should be read by all the low-voltage, risk averse buffoons who are supposed to advise and govern this, once fearless, country.

...

27th June 2020

[Following the Black Lives Matter campaign and the defacing of statues the Archbishop felt the need to reconsider the image of Christ. Best left well alone in my view.]

Why does the Archbishop of Canterbury propose to re-assess Christ's image for He was not born a black African? Another thought, will the Sistine Chapel, for example, now be obliged to paint over Michelangelo's *The Creation of Adam* as both God and Adam are depicted as white.

...

11th March 2017

[Cambridge undergraduates complaining about their food.]

What is wrong with Cambridge undergraduates? At Grenoble University in the late 1950s early 1960s we used to catch, then eat, the pigeons in Place Victor Hugo. This was free and delicious food although *les flics* took a dim view, but outwitting them each evening was also part of the enjoyment - and learning process!

…

29th June 2014

[From Patricia Tailyour, puzzled why someone at Wimbledon only had half a seat! I wonder if she knew the person on the other half?]

Like Veronica Bliss (letters, June 28) I, too, had a wonderful day at Wimbledon last Monday.

However, unlike your correspondent, I had both halves of a very comfortable Centre Court seat with two inches to spare either side: so, I puzzle over why she had only half a seat.

…

22nd October 2015

[Comments on Mr Cameron's waistcoat.]

Mr Cameron was also wearing a soft shirt beneath his white tie: an even worse sartorial error than the exposure of an inch of waistcoat.

…

14th January 2012

[Fears of Scottish devolution.]

We should all be equally as worried about the removal of the Scottish Saltire from the Union Flag.

At a brief count, and including the United Kingdom, ten countries have the Union Flag as part of their national emblem. I dread the day a mere red and white 'Union Jack' flies over Westminster or appears on the white ensigns of the Royal Navy as well as those of the Royal Australian and Royal New Zealand navies.

…

28th January 2021

Paul Warrener in his letter (January 28) thanks God that we are not in a shooting war or the woke BBC would have surrendered last year. The BBC has 'form' in this matter. If he casts his mind back to 1982 he will remember that the BBC - keen for us to lose the Falklands - announced to the world, and Argentina in particular, that the 2nd Battalion the Parachute Regiment was advancing on Goose Green.

…

25th March 2022

[Following an article describing the 'super' yacht and extolling the virtues of an on-board billiards table.]

I wonder how often the guests on board the yacht *Scheherazade* (allegedly owned by Putin) get the chance to play billiards when at sea? The billiards room must be gimballed?

…

4th November 2016

[Following comments about Enid Bytom's writing, using this book as an example.]

Did the artist for the book *Five on a Treasure Island* (Letters November 2) really mean the dinghy to go round in circles to starboard?

...

4th July 2020

[Comments on the exploitation of working dogs.]

What about the thousands of labradors and retrievers (especially the black ones!) that spend all their working lives picking up dead pheasants? In practice, as with so many other 'working' animals, they enjoy it almost more than their owners.

...

11th July 2023

[Thankfully, no picture available!]

Is it really is necessary for Jo's Cervical Cancer Trust to rename the vagina as a 'bonus hole' (Celia Waldon). Surely, without too much difficulty, they could have come up with a more exotic name? I can think of many examples but 'glory hole' and 'the promised land' stand out!

...

3rd July 2016

[Repost to a letter accusing the Brexit vote of having been rigged.]

I have never read such a thoroughly nasty, spiteful and wholly un-British letter as that written by Jeremy Harmer in today's *Daily Telegraph.*

The 52% of those who elected to leave the EU voted, quite simply (and heedless of the regrettably-normal electioneering practices exercised by all sides in every election or referendum) to be governed by a democratically elected parliament within a constitutional monarchy.

What is 'ugly' about that? What is to 'hate' (an unpleasant word at the best of times) about that?

...

15th May 2020

[A Covid poem by Ann D Stevenson.]

On Wednesday last I received this poem from a lady friend, wife of a Royal Marines major-general. Rather fun don't you think?

Isolation

Information, education
Of the present situation.
Population intimidation
More pontification
Stay in location
No integration
No vacation
No celebration
Just segregation
Separation
For stimulation
And inspiration
Use imagination
Conversation
Communication

No virus medication
For rehabilitation
So despite deprivation
Desperation, irritation,
Frustration
And temptation
Avoid dissemination,
Annihilation
Obliteration and damnation
Show consideration
No procrastination
Stay in isolation
And save the nation

PS
Latest information
Outdoor recreation
Oh the jubilation!

A.D.S

…

May 2015

This may be a naïve question (I am a retired Royal Marine and not, praise the Lord, a politician) but if a mortgage company was to contribute, say, four fifths towards the value of my house while also holding the deeds, why should I pay any mansion tax?

...

Published

28th July 2019

[Followed by a personal apology from Christopher Howes, the letters editor, for the newspaper, wrongly describing the wearing of an ensign!]

It may be a small semantic point but one that I cannot help thinking will have the approval of Jacob Rees-Mogg. Ships' ensigns - whether red, white or blue - are always 'worn' and not flown'. (Letters, July 27)

...

26th September 2020

[Sergeant Ratana was shot dead by a man who was in custody.]

I trust we will now see Lewis Hamilton kneel in tribute to police Sergeant Matiu Ratana while football teams hold a one minute silence.

...

21st February 2021

[Comments on appropriate royal names.]

I was not surprised to learn that the newest royal baby is to be christened August for this is an established royal name. In 1934 my mother, then aged 18, enrolled at Göttingen University to read medicine during which time she became 'unofficially' engaged to Ernst August, Prince of Hanover, Duke of Brunswick whose father, a descendant of George III, had been called Augustus. Shortly after his birth in 1914, August was made a British prince by King George V (his godfather) and was heir to the titles Duke of Cumberland and Teviotdale and Earl of Armagh: these were later suspended under the Titles Deprivation Act of 1917.

My mother's departure from Germany in 1937, after just three years of study, was brought forward unexpectedly by the Foreign Office who did not consider it a good thing for the daughter of a Royal Navy captain to be so attached! Nevertheless they continued to correspond (and meet, after the war) until my mother's death in 1971, following which August came to her Thanksgiving Service in Chelsea. However, the point of all this is that neither she nor his friends ever called him Ernst or August but always 'Johnnie'.

...

28th January 2021

[The badger huggers were out in force.]

Vaccinating badgers will do nothing for the safety of ground nesting birds such as skylarks, nor baby hares, hedgehogs, frogs and all the others that make up these pests' diet. Nor will vaccination stop them ruining our fields on which sheep graze. Last year we lost two thirds of the grass on two fields thanks to their rootling. We have also had bovine TB in the past Cull theses vermin now!

...

24th April 2023

[Correspondence about Balkan Sobranie cigarettes.]

Talking of Sobranie cigarettes, during my three un-accompanied postings to the Middle East during the 1960s (45 Commando, Royal Marines, in Aden, HMS *Wizard* in the Persian Gulf and The Sultan of Muscat's Armed Forces) my mother would send a periodical Fortnum's hamper which always contained, *inter alia*, a hefty tin of Balkan Sobranie pipe tobacco and *Playboy* magazine. My fellow officers awaited the hamper's arrival every bit as much as I did.

These days, with smoking *verboten* plus access to the internet I guess all the hamper would contain now would be the tins of smoked mussels and jars of potted shrimps.

...

11th September 2021

I would rather have a picture of Napoléon (despite his attitude towards Britain) on one of our stamps (Letters Martin Davies September 11) rather than unedifying characters from a child's comic. When I asked the post mistress (can I call her that?) why there were only four, first-class stamps in a six-stamp book I had just purchased she, apologetically, asked me to look closer. Who on earth can I send this rubbish to?

...

25th September 2021

I am no cricketer and so really do not mind what the person, of either sex, wielding a bat is called. However, in light of the recent correspondence, I see that that great authority on the sport, Henry Blofeld, writing in this month's *The Oldie*, describes Don Bradman as the 'most successful batter of them all'.

At sea I hope the woke brigade will not force me to call the helmsman 'the helmer'

...

Published

23rd November 2016

Why do the As, Bs and Cs get all the best gales. Could the Meteorological Office please begin next year's storms with Zebedee and then work backwards through the alphabet?

...

13th September 2017

If, as I have suggested in vain, the Meteorological Office named the winter storms starting with Z, X and then Y we might actually reach Storm Trump quite soon.

...

2nd November 2020

On 23rd November 2016 you kindly published my suggestion that the Met Office should name its storms each winter starting with Zebedee and then working backwards. Had they heeded my proposition we would be fast approaching Storm Trump or even Storm Thunberg - which might please her. As it is, Storm Greta cannot be far off - or maybe we have already missed the chance: depending whether or not Storm Jorge is pronounced the Spanish way or the British way.

...

Published

29th September 2022

[Following an announcement that, 'to help the elderly' feet and inches may again be used.]

I am so glad that I can, at last, measure my ropes' circumference in inches and not their diameter in centimetres. I can now bring my brass and wood measuring device out of retirement.

...

30th August 2021

[Nowzad Dogs is a British-based animal welfare charity. It was created by Pen Farthing, a former Royal Marines commando, after rescuing a dog he called Nowzad while serving in the town of Nowzad in Afghanistan.]

I smiled at your page 16 cartoon (below) this morning while thinking that here was a prime candidate for 'Pen' Farthing's Nowzad abandoned dogs centre.

...

28th October 2022

I doubt that the Just Stop Oil eco-terrorists, selfishly disrupting innocent lives, have the intelligence to realise that their 'weapon of choice', super glue, is partially a by-product of petroleum. This superb irony is clearly beyond their wit to appreciate!

...

24th June 2023

[Correspondence on when to turn off the Aga - or not.]

We turn off our Aga during the summer as we do not need the bottom oven for drying the evening's kindling.

...

28th July 2021

[What's in a nickname?]

I know nothing of Aunt Mary's Bottom or of Hetty Pegler's Tump but I do know that sailors call Weston-super-Mare 'Aggie on Horseback' after Dame Agnes Weston who founded her popular sailors' rest homes. Likewise the sloop HMS *Weston.*

...

28th June 2023

If the ladies want their own Ashes series against Australia, to avoid confusion, they could call it the Cinders (*pace* Cinderella).

...

Published

1st July 1992

Following on from Lord Lewin's formation of the urgently needed National Ships Preservation Committee (report May 18) and the subsequent correspondence (May 28) there are a few more deserving cases 'on the books' of the World Ship Trust at the moment than the *Queen Mary*.

The *Queen Mary Foundation* in California has just told me that with the impending loss of the Walt Disney company as her present manager the future of this greatest of all ocean liners is about to rest in the none-too-sure hands of the port of Long Beach.

While the city of Long Beach says it intends to find a successor to the Disney company it has never been an active supporter of the *Queen Mary* and is now of the opinion that a more likely alternative is to scrap the ship.

By Septembers it may be too late to save a ship that, were he still alive, would have been very much in John Masefield's mind when he ended his poem 'Ships' with the words:

> *They mark our passage as a race of men,*
> *Earth will not see such ships as those again.*

Tragically, quotes from Rupert Brooke's poem 'The Soldier' are likely to be more relevant.

Chairman, the World Ship Trust.

RMS Queen Mary in Long Beach, California

…

Published

23rd July 1989

Mr Ian Gillis and Mr Peter Lyons (Letters, July 18, 20) need lament no more. Britain can, and should, preserve her 18th century wrecks on British soil - at Port Stanley.

The wrecks of the Falkland Islands belong to the islanders (except in a very few cases) and should not be at the beck and call of any outside party no matter how worthy their cause.

The Falkland climate, devoid of acids in the air and trees with wood-destroying spores coupled with the near constant drying wind, is the most ideal place for these brave ships to remain.

The cost of removal, as we saw in the internationally deserving case of the SS *Great Britain*, is prohibitive. It would be far better to spend this money on stabilizing and preserving them in their present positions. The chances of the islanders agreeing to the removal of any wreck is slim for the *Fennia* experience still hurts. She was towed away in the mid-1970s shortly before her 'saviours' ran out of money and she was broken up for scrap in South America.

The islanders should now make some of their own funds available for preservation. Interested parties from abroad could, perhaps, sponsor vessels in which they have a national, historical or previous commercial interest.

The islanders can then build up a matchless collection of ships which will be preserved closer to their natural element than would be the case in any northern museum.

There are, too, other reasons for them to be kept where they lie. They are as much part of the Falkland scenery as the tussock-grass or diddle-dee. Many had second careers with the wool industry as storage sheds and some were repaired only to return after another encounter with an iceberg or a grey-beard of Cape Horn.

These ships are as firmly embedded in the folklore of the islands as the digging of peat or the ranching of sheep. They are part of the Falklands heritage and must remain so.

The SS Great Britain in Sparrow Cove, Falkland Islands, in the late 1960s

...

18th December 2019

[Following an article about underpants being made from bamboo.]

So far all your correspondents have been male. Maybe the ladies are too shy to admit that they, too, do not like the thought of bamboo knickers.

...

4th January 2019

[Mr Packham had offered to lay a trail for a pack of foxhounds.]

What a pity Mr Packham did not offer his services to a pack of bloodhounds. The Master might have accepted.

Bloodhound

...

12th July 2014

[Complaints about the cost of travel per mile.]

Richard Coleman complains about the price of a skiff between Texas and Mexico (Letters, July 11). I wonder if he has used Bristol airport where a luggage trolley costs £2 - non-returnable? As the distance between terminal and the dropping off/collecting point is less than one hundred yards this works out at £36 per mile - and you have to provide your own motive power!

...

4th August 2017

[Discussions on homosexuals in the armed forces.]

I know that I am not the only member of my generation who is heartily relieved that I left the armed forces before homosexuality was made compulsory.

...

5th August 2017

[National Trust to support homosexual marriages.]

If the Director-General of the National Trust really wanted to 'make everyone feel welcome' then she should not have promoted 'either side'. Regardless of the law, many of us still regard sodomy/buggery as an offensive act.

...

13th July 2016

[Discussions on the Cameron legacy.]

Mr Cameron's unfortunate legacy includes the right for sodomites to marry. Thankfully I left the Royal Marines before he made buggery compulsory!

...

Published

11th June 2023

I recently purchased two Ukraine/United Kingdom lapel badges. Guess where they were made - China!

…

14th March 2021

Considering that it was allegedly one of their own kind that abducted and murdered Sarah Everard there was an even greater need for the police to have acted with the utmost circumspection, not to say care and sympathy. Instead, they have shamed us all.

…

12th November 2016

I wonder which syllable in the word democracy it is that the Lib Dems cannot accept.

…

1st December 2021

[Correspondence about school reports.]

My final English report, after four years at the wonderful prep-school Stubbington House, read *Ewen is too much of a dilettante and a lazy one at that.* I've never looked back!

…

1st January 2013

Andrew Pierce is correct (Letters January 1): national honours should recognize courage (military and civilian, physical and moral) and those genuinely good deeds that are beyond the call of everyday citizenship.

Might I suggest, therefore, that Olympic medal winners are, formally, allowed to add a more relevant post-nominal that would publically indicate their achievement: for example OGM - Olympic Gold Medallist, OSM - Olympic Silver Medallist and OBM - Olympic Bronze Medallist.

This would be unarguable: it would also negate unseemly mutterings about who got what and who deserved what in the national honours list.

...

5th April 2020

[And more thoughts on honouring the NHS and others.]

When this whole ghastly affair (Covid) is over I pray that the Government will pay tribute to all those who have helped in a special honours and awards list as is the case when the armed forces return from operations: it must not be mixed in with the standard bi-annual lists. I would pray, too, that it is produced quickly for those who have risked their lives on an hourly basis. They will have come closer to death, and more often in such a comparatively short period than many of us who served for years in the navy, army or air force.

If sporting teams can be honoured swiftly - too swiftly - then so can representatives of the National Health Service and the emergency services while not forgetting those who have kept us fed, transported, supplied, watched over and, yes, those who have delivered goods in their white vans as well as those who have taken away our rubbish.

...

9th August 2021

While I am full of praise for all our Olympians - medal winners or not - I wonder if an 'automatic' MBE or OBE is the correct award. If all medal winners were allowed to use the post-nominals OGM, OSM or OBM (Olympic Gold Medallist and so on) would this not more accurately, and more visibly, (even, more proudly) reflect their achievements?

...

21st May 2020

[Yet more thoughts on honours for the NHS.]

We are told that this year's Queen's Birthday Honours List has been postponed from June to the autumn so that those involved with the treatment of Covid-19 can be included.

I do not believe this to be right as there is a danger of the list becoming unbalanced for both the 'normal' recipients as well as those from the health and support services.

Surely, under such extreme circumstances, the government should establish a special honours and awards list as is the case when the armed forces return from operations: it must not be mixed in with the standard bi-annual list.

...

20th August 2016

Edward Cartner is spot on (Letters, August 20). Furthermore national honours should recognize courage (military and civilian, physical and moral) and those genuinely good deeds that are beyond the call of everyday citizenship: nor do I see the value in being awarded a medal for having won a medal.

Might I suggest, therefore, that Olympic medal winners are, formally, allowed to add a more relevant post-nominal to their names that would publically and internationally indicate their sporting achievement: for example OGM - Olympic Gold Medallist; OSM - Olympic Silver Medallist and OBM - Olympic Bronze Medallist.

...

8th April 2020

[Discussions on how to honour the NHS nurses and doctors.]

When our armed forces return from a successful campaign abroad - and few military operations, if any in recent years, have matched the widespread perils of this current devastation - they are accorded their own specific and lengthy honours and awards list. I pray that those who are keeping us safe, fed and supplied will receive a similar accolade. It would be a travesty if their names were simply added to the bi-annual lists of worthy, but far from heroic, recipients.

. . .

14th April 2020

[Yet more discussions on how to honour the NHS.]

The Florence Nightingale Medal is awarded for "exceptional courage and devotion to the wounded, sick or disabled or to civilian victims of a conflict or disaster" or "exemplary services or a creative and pioneering spirit in the areas of public health or nursing education."

I cannot think of a more appropriate recognition for those demonstrating supreme gallantry while at the greatest risk to themselves.

. . .

30th August 2017

[FLOTUS v FLUK]

Seeing the acronym on Mrs Trump's baseball hat (below) made me thank God that the United Kingdom's First Lady will never choose to do the same!

…

25th November 2022

[Comments on a suggestion that sunset, or 'five bells', is the best time to start the evening's drinking.]

I admire Craig Heeley's drinking habits. Here, in South Devon, sunset tonight is at 1619 and 'five bells' will be struck rather earlier, when working a dog watch system, at 1430. Even for a Royal Marine that is a touch too soon for the first G&T. Ignoring the two dog watches 'five bells' at 1830 strikes me (and certainly my wife) as a more reasonable time to start the evening - regardless of when the sun sets.

…

2nd May 2020

[The BBC's bias.]

I agree wholeheartedly with David Palfreyman (Letters May 2) which is why yesterday I signed a petition that read in part:

'The BBC is politically biased, constantly projecting fear into the community during this pandemic. It is appalling to listen to BBC programmes where the presenters use arrogant and aggressive tones as they ask negative questions, while employing the benefit of hindsight to undermine the unrelenting and positive work of the Government.'

I would encourage all decent people who would prefer to watch, or listen to, our publically funded national broadcaster telling the un-biased truth to log on to https://www.change.org/StopBBCbias and sign the petition.

...

5th May 2020

[People commenting on the lack of erudite books on Mr Gove's bookshelf.]

I looked for one of my books on Mr Gove's book shelve but in vain so I guess I shall just have to keep on writing.

Surely a well-balanced library is to be admired not condemned? I have accounts written by both British and Argentine authors from 1982 and am far better informed as a result.

...

18th May 2017

[Flight safety.]

Tom Boyd-Smith had his plastic corkscrew confiscated for fear it might be used to 'take control of an aircraft'. (Letters May 18) On the first day of the 'commando course' phase of our Royal Marines training Colour Sergeant Alexander held up his much-scarred hands with the statement, "Gentlemen, forget for a moment the Fairburn-Sykes fighting knife, let me introduce you to the two most dangerous weapons you will ever carry." Over the next weeks we were taught eleven ways of killing or maiming an opponent with nothing but our bare hands. I wonder how Schiphol security will counter this obvious breach of security.

...

13th February 2013

[The *Daily Telegraph* of February 12 showed a black shadow of one of President Hollande's hands across Mrs Obama's left breast!]

Bearing in mind François Hollande's reputation it strikes me that he can't even control his own shadow!

François Hollande and the Obamas wave from the Truman Balcony during a state ceremony at the White House to mark the French president's arrival

...

22nd April 2018

Gary Streeter Esq., MP,

AREAS OF OUTSTANDING NATURAL BEAUTY

We live on the edge of, and overlook, an AONB in the South Hams.

In yesterday's *Western Morning News*, and in a recent CPRE newsletter, we have learned of the likelihood that swathes of this protected land are in danger of being built over. This is, apparently, to help solve the housing crisis and yet we also read that houses already available in less desirable locations are difficult to sell. Just because they are more easy to sell should, most emphatically, not be an excuse for the government to condone the building of houses in beautiful, and legally protected, countryside.

A number of other points are raised. The first is that most of these are likely to be second homes (thus hardly easing the national situation) and, second, what is wrong with the many acres of brown-field sites (especially those within the confines of Plymouth city) that would become attractive to developers if the relevant VAT was reduced or, even more sensibly, abolished?

We are particularly disturbed by the loss of the AONB having *the highest status of protection in relation to landscape and scenic beauty* to be replaced, if we read this correctly, by the (purposefully ambiguous?) proposal that *major developments will only be allowed in exceptional circumstances.* Who decides what is a major development and who decides what are circumstances so exceptional that they involve the, *de facto*, destruction of beautiful, formally-protected countryside? Five new houses within an urban setting is minor but on a virgin, coastal hillside it would most certainly be major. *Scenic beauty* is the main pillar for the AONB's existence so what rationale lies behind the removal of this fundamental caveat.

It strikes us that a healthy measure of common-sense needs to be applied before these changes in the AONB's status are implemented, coupled with an understanding of the countryside that always seems to be absent among urban MPs in Westminster. The potential loss of productive farmland will also be an irreversible consequence, as we have witnessed with that other misuse of the countryside - the solar panel.

...

2nd August 2015

[Written during the search for the missing Malaysian airliner.]

There has to be a reason why an aircraft's 'black box' (below) is not fitted with an hydrostatic release that is activated at a certain depth. The flight and cockpit voice recorders can then float on the ocean's surface: all the way to Reunion if necessary.

I wonder what it is.

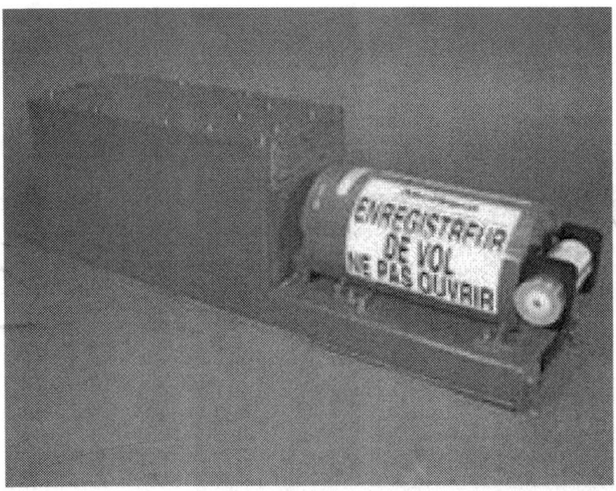

...

11th January 2022

To find someone not guilty on the rather spurious excuse that it will prevent them becoming a short-term martyr - as Esther Rantzen seems to suggest - is hardly the correct application of justice as I understand it.

...

25th September 2010

[Following a similar report.]

One evening in the wardroom of HMS *Drake* a Second Officer Wrens put her head round the door to ask, "Has anyone seen Mike Hunt." Gallantly, no one answered.

...

31st December 2018

[Comment on a report about the French reaction to the channel migrants.]

What would Nelson do? Simple, welcome them all, men women and children, with open arms. The more the merrier to help man his fleet in the seemingly-unceasing 'war' with France. It would also relieve the press-gangs of their necessary but distasteful task. Positive results all round!

...

12th July 2017

[Reports on the expression 'a *niga* in the wood pile'.]

This fabricated nonsense is about a pile of wooden tally sticks called *nigas* – or so we were taught, aged six in 1948, at the US Marine Corps school in Quantico, Virginia.

...

21st June 2017

[During a discussion arguing whether or not there are any 'balanced' and UK-friendly nations in the Middle East.]

The Sultanate of Oman.

...

15th November 2023

Lieutenant-Colonel John Wyatt (Letters November 15) states that his grandfather's cousin, Brigadier General Louis John Wyatt, reported that, on the night of November 7 1920, the bodies of four unidentified ***soldiers*** were brought to the hut that served as the chapel of the town Saint-Pol-sur-Ternoise.

Presumably, if they were unidentified, it is a fair assumption that the units of the four men were also unknown. This is relevant for the Unknown Warrior might not have been a soldier but a sailor or Royal Marine - members of the 63rd Royal Naval Division that fought at Arras, Ancre, the Somme, Ypres and Passchendaele - or, indeed, an aviator of the Royal

Flying Corps, many of whom also perished above those mud-filled trenches.

Rightly, we shall never know.

...

17th March 2019

In a letter to my MP, Gary Streeter, I complained, *inter alia*, about the arrogant, xenophobic, only-we-know-best attitude of our parliamentarians. His reply is revealing: *I am sorry but there is no one at Westminster who agrees with your point of view.* Of course not for therein lies the problem as, I suspect, 60 million others agree with me!

...

18th October 2018

[Following a woke complaint about the use of the word 'gentlemen' and the de-sexing of names.]

Patum Peperium. The Gentleman's Relish?

. . .

19th January 2021

[Correspondence suggesting the word 'black' should not be used in certain circumstances.]

I own a sailing vessel called *Black Velvet*...what are my chances of being challenged by the Border Force when next we are allowed afloat?

. . .

10th March 2021

[Following Meghan Markle's accusation of racism in the royal family. One of many similar letters.]

I can find nothing at all offensive or racist in an attempt to predict an unborn child's colour or, indeed, its sex. I know a number of couples whose offspring have married mixed-race partners when the mounting excitement during the nine month was often enhanced by light hearted and harmless banter on these two unknowns. Indeed, we would have been surprised if these perfectly acceptable subjects had not been discussed.

…

17th August 2017

[Rees-Mogg was accused of not knowing the price of a pint of milk.]

Does Jacob Rees-Mogg know the price of a pint of milk? With six children, I am certain he must do.

…

25th April 2021

I am full of admiration for Mr Ian Rivers and his attempt to row west to east across the North Atlantic single-handed and wish him God speed.

However, he should be grateful that your reporter, Dominic Nicholls, is not responsible for the passage planning. The route Mr Rivers plans, from New York to the Isles of Scilly, is not 'the wrong way'. The prevailing winds in that part of the North Atlantic also blow from west to east while the Gulf Stream could push Mr Rivers towards his destination at roughly 70 nautical miles per day. Furthermore, tropical storms in the North Atlantic, although not unknown, are most rare.

Finally, Mr Nicholls makes much of the fact that navigation will by sextant as though this was a rare phenomenon. This fool-proof method of determining a vessel's position has been conducted by mariners for hundreds of years, so, *bravo* to Ian Rivers for choosing the most reliable navigational instrument available and the most sensible route.

…

9th September 2023

[Following the headline: *More than 100 British families pledge to make slavery reparations.*]

I doubt that there is a family in the land, white, black, Arab or oriental, whose ancestors did not benefit from, or who were not involved in - as a consumer, tradesman, ship owner, employee or merchant - the slave trade. On that basis every single one of us should be shunned for the behaviour of our forebears and not just those whose works live through statues, paintings and museum artefacts.

Commodities, all vital for the improvement of life across every social 'class', were, rightly or wrongly - but inevitably - produced and brought to the British Isles largely thanks to the employment of slaves and coolies: sugar and rum from the West Indies; salt from the Mediterranean; frankincense from the Middle East; cotton and tobacco from the Americas and East Africa; spices from the Orient; tea from India and East Africa; coffee from the Yemen; jute, hemp and sisal from West Africa; wines from France and Portugal; timber from the Baltic; gold and guano for the land from South America: the list goes on. Those who profited from the slave trade were also able to acquire property across the United Kingdom and thus employ many who would otherwise have been destitute.

Whether we like it or not, whether we approve or not, without the slave trade feeding our insatiable need for 'consumer goods' and food we would have remained in the middle ages.

Impressment into the Royal Navy was, too, a form of slavery but without which this country's wealth, success in battle and thus security of the homeland coupled to global influence would not have been possible.

Of course slavery was and remains abhorrent, but it happened and is, sadly, still happening in one form or another in less enlightened states.

…

30th November 2020

[Much the same. Reparations for past slavery.]

Let alone the hypocrisy, it beggars belief that some continue to blame the mistakes of the past on subsequent generations.

I doubt that there is a family in the land, of any colour or persuasion, whose ancestors did not benefit from, or who were not involved in - as a consumer, tradesman, ship owner, planter or merchant - the slave trade. On that basis every single one of us should be shunned for the behaviour of our forebears and not just those whose works live through statues, paintings and museum artefacts.

Commodities, all vital for the improvement of life across every social 'class', were, rightly or wrongly - but inevitably - produced and brought to the British Isles thanks to the employment of slaves and coolies: sugar from the West Indies; salt from the Mediterranean; frankincense from the Middle East; cotton and tobacco from the Americas and East Africa; spices from the Orient; tea from India and East Africa; coffee from the Yemen; jute, hemp and sisal from West Africa; wines from France and Portugal; timber from the Baltic; gold and guano for the land from South America. The list goes on.

Whether we like it or not, whether we approve or not, without the slave trade - which sometimes worked in both directions - feeding our insatiable need for, then, 'consumer goods' we would have remained in the middle ages.

Impressment into the Royal Navy was, too, a form of slavery but without which this country's commercial wealth and success in battle would not have been possible.

Of course slavery was and remains abhorrent, but it happened and is, sadly, still happening in one form or another in less enlightened states.

...

19th November 2021

Grey squirrels are nothing more than bushy-tailed, tree rats (Letters November 19) and should be treated as such to avoid the destruction of trees and the decimation of, *inter alia*, frogs and birds eggs. In 40 years our three walnut trees have produced just two nuts thanks to *Sciurus carolinenses.*

On this farm they are shot.

...

2nd September 2022

Tomorrow (September 3) is Merchant Navy Day as proclaimed by His Majesty George V in recognition of the sacrifices made during the First World War, often unsung, usually unknown and that continue in conflicts to this day. That evening I shall greet supper with the grace that was said at the Nautical College, Pangbourne in the 1950s: *For what we are about to eat, thank God and the Merchant Fleet.*

...

Published

6th November 2018

[Considered on Facebook to have been the most pointless letter of the month! I agree!]

When sunbathing - a rather vulgar Italian habit that I enjoy - I do not wear a tie. More seriously, a tie is necessary to add colour and individuality to an otherwise rather boring selection of men's formal suits. The ladies are luckier for they can change the combinations of colour and degrees of formality almost hourly: and what a joy that is!

The other occasion that a tie is less sartorially important but of vital practicality is when sailing in high latitudes. A tightly knotted Royal Cruising Club tie is the only method I have found to be all-but fool proof for preventing icy water creeping down ones back. A soggy towel freezes against the skin adding to the discomfort and, possibly, the danger of frostbite.

...

Unknown date

[The Prime Minister expressed concerns that we should beware of leaving the EU for then the UK would be entering 'uncharted waters'.]

We are at a loss to understand why Mrs May in particular, and Remainers in general, should be using the fear of 'uncharted waters' as one of the excuses for finding it difficult to leave the EU. It was the very taming of such regions, then most of the globe, that made this country the greatest trading and military nation in history. Across four centuries the way ahead was paved by farsighted politicians and diplomats sponsoring gallant ships' companies and courageous explorers on foot, mule and camel. The Northwest passage, an uncharted area (and largely still is) held the key to shorter trading routes to the Far East, but no one baulked at attempting it.

Further afield, India and the East Indies produced spices; the West Indies supplied sugar; South America gave us guano and gold; South Africa offered diamonds; North America taught us to smoke while the inhospitable southern oceans brought us fish oils and whale bones. Wool from Australia, lamb from New Zealand and tea from China arrived despite crossing the most dangerous seas to be found anywhere on earth. Then we 'invented' the industrial revolution and won the prosperity that came with it.

None of these markets existed before intrepid explorers on land and sea, backed by politicians, risk-taking merchant traders, heroic military commanders and the most imaginative of inventors, forged their way across and into 'uncharted territories'. Now new forms of 'uncharted territories' - political, commercial and financial - should, once more, be seen as exciting challenges. Challenges that are waiting to be grasped with open eyes and wide-spread arms and not treated as black holes by those who can see no future outside the waning EU.

Our predecessors took huge financial risks but those audacious actions, performed by a far bolder, more enlightened establishment, made us what we are (or, rather, what we were). Now the lessons learned from four centuries of enterprise are to be forfeited because a timid, morally bankrupt collection of short-sighted politicians are frightened of taking the smallest risk: terrified of failing because they believe that successful endeavor can only be regulated into existence by the dead hand of the EU.

Of course there will be setbacks but the final prize, as our current 'leaders' should have learned by now, will be worth every one of the risks. Facing the challenges of 'uncharted territory' is what we have always done best and is, after all, what most of us voted for.

As we used to say in our adventurous youth, 'bugger the begrudgers, we'll do it our way'.

...

16th August 2020

I admire Rhiane Fatinukun's initiative in setting up Black Girls Hike and wish her all success but…in these all-inclusive days I doubt I would be able to establish an adventure company called White Boys Sail.

…

5th April 2019

[Mrs May pushes for a second Brexit referendum!]

If I may misquote: Never in the field of inept, Machiavellian politics has so much treachery been exercised by so few for the despair of so many.

…

20th September 2014

Will someone please explain why it was necessary to equip the deskbound ballot-counters at the Royal Highland Centre in Edinburgh with 'high visibility vests'?

…

27th July 2015

Glorious, exciting and full of hope as it is there is something strangely bizarre about the British entry for the America's Cup.

In Saturday's pictures the starboard side of the mains'l has the Union Flag upside down, the accepted sign of a disaster at sea… and yet the port side of the sail has it the right way up: assuming, as with the other nations and their mains'ls, the wind blows from for'ard to aft!

After all the money and attention to detail this rather public display of uncertainty will not, I trust, be a pointer to the final result.

…

And again on 22nd July 2016

On the assumption that the wind blows from for'ard to aft on Sir Ben Ainslie's catamaran it is unfortunate that the prominent union flag at the head of the mainsail is flying upside down The photograph of the British America's Cup entry shows quite clearly that the Union Flag at the head of the mains'l's starboard side is either upside down or back to front on the fair assumption that the wind blows from bow to stern. Bizarrely it is correct on the port side of the vessel.

I hope this signal of nautical distress is not a taster for things to come.

…

12th February 2010

I hope that our Olympic Flag carrier in Canada is told to replace the Union Flag the right way up on its pole: on today's BBC lunchtime news it was proudly waved upside down. Someone in the national team should care enough to have checked beforehand: if not then the signalled 'distress' will come as no surprise.

…

26th June 2020

[Following incorrect observations that the union flag was upside down on the national aircraft.]

Of course it is the right way up, assuming the wind on an aeroplane blows from for'ard to aft – but I am not an aviator.

...

11th January 2023

I wish the RAF's Chinooks well for their deployment to Estonia (page 4 photograph) but assuming, even with a helicopter, that the wind blows from for'ard to aft it seems a pity that their Union Flags are upside down. I trust that this will not be an unfortunate omen.

...

Published

31st March 1996

SIR—I recently resigned from the Referendum Party.

The decision was easy to make once I realised that, far from preventing the United Kingdom from becoming even more subsumed by the European Union, the most likely outcome would be to prevent the Conservative Party winning the next general election. Thus, with the election of a party wishing to accede to Europe's wishes would come the result which Sir James says he hopes to prevent.

The destruction of the one party most likely to combat Europe's extremes does not make sense. A referendum, yes! But not during a general election.

EWEN SOUTHBY-TAILYOUR
Ermington, South Devon

…

1st May 2023

Surely Madame Tussauds has got it badly wrong. The waxwork model of Prince Harry shows him smiling when all we ever see is a scowl?

...

Published

27th October 1998

[Following lengthy correspondence suggesting alternative words for the acronyms or names for airlines such as, PIA - Please Inform Allah - or Lufthansa - Let Us Fondle The Hostesses And No One Say Anything.]

Boys Overseas After Crumpet is, roughly, what we called BOAC's pilots in the early Sixties. Watching them in the Crescent Hotel at Steamer Point Aden, or the Speedbird Hotel, Bahrain, it was obvious why.

...

Published

3rd February 2000

[Following complaints from the animal rights lobby about the then Countess of Wessex's fur hat.]

I support the Countess's decision to wear a fox fur hat. What a pity I was unable to counter her critics with a reply I was once forced to make when giving a lecture on sailing through an Arctic winter. As I donned my favourite Arctic-wolf fur hat to demonstrate its thermal properties a strident voice harangued me about animal rights.

When she had stopped I replied quietly "Madam, it was him or me!" and I was able to finish the talk un-heckled.

I shall be wearing it again this summer when at sea north of the Arctic circle.

...

20th February 2002

Sir John Keegan

I read your piece in today's paper with interest as I am writing the biography (actually the autobiography as it is in the first person) of Andre Hue who now has Alzheimer's and cancer. Andre (French father, Welsh mother but English passport so de Gaulle was able to accept his recruitment by SOE 'F' Section) was an eighteen-year-old Englishman lifted out of northern France by MTB in 1944, trained by the SOE and dropped behind the lines on D Day to establish his own circuit, *Hillbilly*. Over the next two months, at the age of nineteen, he was awarded the DSO, the *Croix de Guerre avec Palmes* and made a *Chevalier de la Legion d'Honneur.*

His girlfriend of the time (he wanted to marry her but he was lifted out again for further SOE work in the east of France and eventually in Burma before the 'physical' friendship could blossom into marriage!) helped in many remarkably courageous ways. (All of which are well tabulated and will be covered in the book, *The Next Moon*.) Although he tried he never achieved even an MBE for her: Genevieve Pondard is still alive and I hope to meet her this autumn.

I absolutely agree that the women - and all the others - who served with SOE in Europe should be 'advanced' and I would support you wholeheartedly if you intend taking that 'campaign' further!

When I was serving in the Royal Marines and, subsequently, with the FCO in Bosnia, there was always the Imperial Service Medal (ISM) for rewarding very minor or very junior civil servants for their long service and good conduct. On the demise of the BEM and the consequent use of the MBE for postmistresses, lollipop ladies and road sweepers I could not fathom out why the ISM was not used instead - as it always had been. When we felt that, for instance, the civilian range warden who had clocked up forty years of fine service deserved some public recognition it was the ISM for which the citation was written - and with which he was presented by the Lord Lieutenant or General in much the same way as the BEM was actually pinned on to a well-deserving, but junior military chest. What has happened to the ISM I wonder, for it was/is the ideal 'medal' which would prevent (it has to be said - worthy though they no doubt are) the devaluing of the civilian MBE.

...

8th March 2003

[Replying to a letter to all members asking for their views on allowing ladies to use all the club rooms thus leaving the men no place to 'hide'! I did not win my argument.]

The Chairman, Army and Navy Club

I write in response to your letter of the February 11. I am most emphatically not in favour of altering club rules in respect of lady members using the Smoking Room and the Smoking Room Bar. I cannot accept that politically correct 'equal opportunities' have any place in a 'private' officers' club, not least of all that the rules will now be tilted in favour of the lady members as officers will not be able to use the comforts of the Ladies Drawing Room unless accompanied (quite rightly) by a lady - in effect, therefore, the ladies are now the dominant factor. The Rag really should be the last bastion of defence against the relentless march of such modern-day idiocies!

This whole thing smacks of some few agitating women members (civilians I wonder - or from the more strident faction of commissioned ladies) who must have known the traditions of this ancient establishment when they applied for membership. I adore women!...but it is nice to escape their presence just every so often and one's London Club has to be the place for such brief escapism.

Please do not allow the feminine influence to take charge.

...

Published

following a telephone interview.

29th April 2002

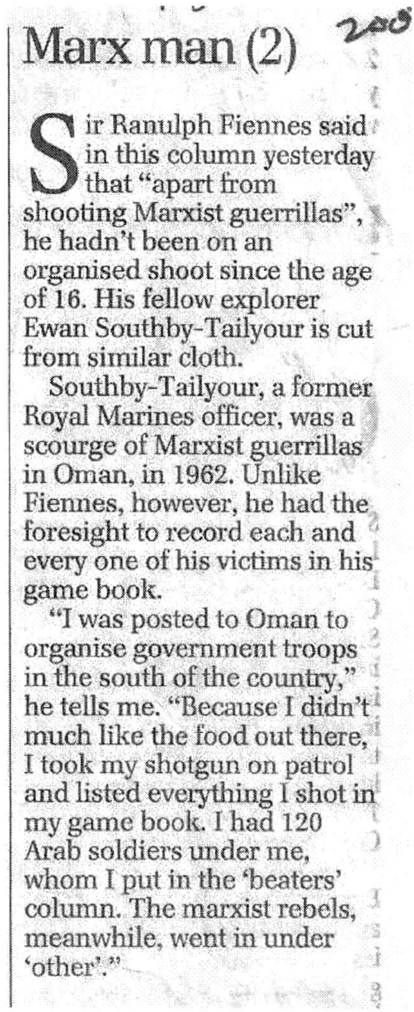

Marx man (2)

Sir Ranulph Fiennes said in this column yesterday that "apart from shooting Marxist guerrillas", he hadn't been on an organised shoot since the age of 16. His fellow explorer Ewan Southby-Tailyour is cut from similar cloth.

Southby-Tailyour, a former Royal Marines officer, was a scourge of Marxist guerrillas in Oman, in 1962. Unlike Fiennes, however, he had the foresight to record each and every one of his victims in his game book.

"I was posted to Oman to organise government troops in the south of the country," he tells me. "Because I didn't much like the food out there, I took my shotgun on patrol and listed everything I shot in my game book. I had 120 Arab soldiers under me, whom I put in the 'beaters' column. The marxist rebels, meanwhile, went in under 'other'."

The Daily Mail's diarist reported much the same and although true I remember saying no such thing!

…

Published

27th March 2006

Your front page photograph (March 27) proves why we are better off with a monarch rather than a president.

[Not once but twice!]

. . .

28th March 2021

[General Welch was imprisoned for boarding school allowance fraud.]

What a shame the court martial that found Major-General Welch guilty of fraud did not sit in judgement on those MPs caught in the expenses scandal: a good many of them did not lose their reputations; did not go to prison for 21 months and were not required to pay back the sums they had falsely claimed. Most significantly no member was retrospectively dismissed and thus did not lose a handsome parliamentary pension. Some simply resigned or were suspended with only a handful serving a prison sentence, one even returning to the House of Lords on release. None of these were options open to the general.

…

9th August 2023

[Complaint that there are no good, small estate cars.]

Frances Harding should look no further than the smaller Škoda Yeti. Not only do the back seats fold forwards but they can also be removed altogether. My petrol version is ULEZ compatible, is square-ended and the right size for our bucolic needs.

…

21st October 2023
Trafalgar Day

About three weeks ago a smart, modern car was dumped (stolen?) in a gateway just off the A38, a few miles east of Plymouth. Yesterday I noticed a Traffic Officer's Range Rover parked alongside so I stopped to tell the 'officer' that it had been there for well over two weeks and that I was delighted to see that action was being taken. "Oh no," he said, "I'm parked here to check my emails. My responsibility is purely the A38, so you will need to report this to the police yourself." "Why can't you do that?" I replied, "You must be in permanent touch with the police." He repeated that it was not his job to report such matters as it was off the dual carriageway. What on earth are traffic officers for and is there no commons sense or even collective responsibility within these organisations?

…

8th October 2023

Surely Simon McIlroy must know that 'behind the bike sheds' has always been the preferred rendezvous for that first illicit kiss rather than a forbidden cigarette. Far more satisfying – and tasty!

...

9th June 2023

[Charles Smith-Jones asked when it started to all go wrong for Harry and Meghan.]

Charles Smith-Jones knows the answer to his two questions as well as the rest of us - St George's Chapel, Windsor Castle, on the 19th May 2018.

...

30th October 2023

[Following lengthy discussions on Harold Wilson's mistress.]

In October 1968 Harold Wilson and Marcia Williams had near-adjoining cabins on board HMS *Fearless* at Gibraltar for the talks with Ian Smith over Rhodesia. One evening she and Gerald Kaufman were late back from a 'run ashore' and complaining that the naval staff car had not waited four hours for them outside a restaurant.

Arriving around midnight Ms Williams was so angry that she stormed past the Royal Marines sentry guarding the Prime Minister' sleeping quarters to protest.

Later the Royal Marine was on a charge for allowing Harold Wilson to be disturbed but he had already had his revenge for when Marcia Williams eventually returned to her own cabin and laid down on the bunk it suddenly reverted to its daytime role as a sofa, squashing her horizontally against the bulkhead. The marine waited a very long time indeed before responding to her squeals.

This incident took mere seconds to be 'broadcast' throughout the ship, thus enhancing the long-rife rumours of 'an affair'!

...

8th October 2020

[Following sadness on the (temporary) demise of the biscuits.]

What am I bid for my last, unopened packet of Bath Olivers?

...

4th January 2021

[Discussion on the best cure for a hangover.]

I am unsure which author it was (Kingsley Amis or Evelyn Waugh?) who wrote that the perfect cure for a hangover was the 'vigorous performance of the sexual act'. Perhaps someone can verify this for me.

...

21st June 2016

[Pros and cons on remaining in - or leaving - the European Union.]

I've no idea who wrote this but it seems to sum it all up very neatly:

> 'Won't you join our Common Market?' said the spider to the fly,
> 'It really is a winner and the cost is not too high.
>
> 'I know De Gaulle said 'Non', but he hadn't got a clue,
> 'We want you in, my friends and I, for we have plans for you.
>
> 'You'll have to pay a little more than we do, just for now,
> 'As Herr Kohl said, and I agree, we need a new milch cow.
>
> 'It's just a continental term, believe me, mon ami,
> 'Like 'Vive la France' or 'Mad Anglais' or even 'E.E.C.'.
>
> 'As to the rules, don't worry friend, there's really but a few
> 'You'll find that we ignore them - but they all apply to you.
>
> 'Give and share between us, that's what it's all about,
> 'You do all the giving, and we all share it out.
>
> 'It's very British, is it not, to help a friend in need?
> 'You've done it twice in two World Wars, a fact we must concede.
>
> 'So climb aboard the Market Train, don't sit there on the side,
> 'Your continental cousins want to take you for a ride'

…

8th May 2013

I do not know whether to be surprised or not that Andrew Morton's recent biography of Princess Diana is to be found under the fiction section in my local library.

…

6th December 1992

[Twenty-one years earlier I had also commented.]

You may be interested in the attached clipping from the Books page, fiction section, of yesterday's Western Morning News which shows that not everyone, thank goodness, is taken in by Mr Morton's book!

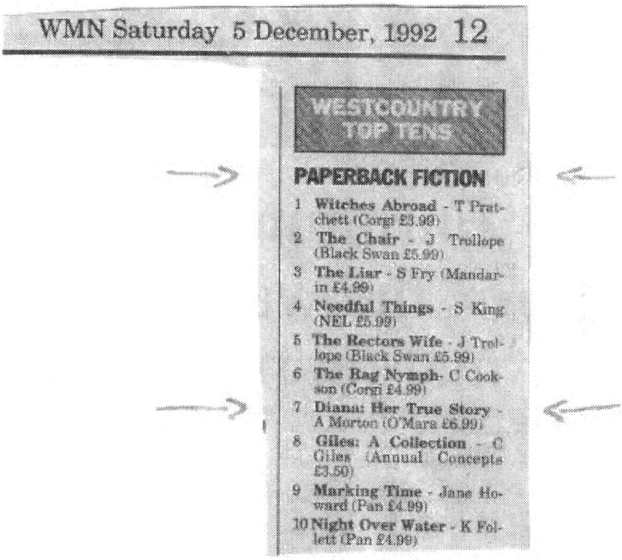

WMN Saturday 5 December, 1992 12

WESTCOUNTRY TOP TENS

PAPERBACK FICTION

1 **Witches Abroad** - T Pratchett (Corgi £3.99)
2 **The Chair** - J Trollope (Black Swan £5.99)
3 **The Liar** - S Fry (Mandarin £4.99)
4 **Needful Things** - S King (NEL £5.99)
5 **The Rectors Wife** - J Trollope (Black Swan £5.99)
6 **The Rag Nymph**- C Cookson (Corgi £4.99)
7 **Diana: Her True Story** - A Morton (O'Mara £6.99)
8 **Giles: A Collection** - C Giles (Annual Concepts £3.50)
9 **Marking Time** - Jane Howard (Pan £4.99)
10 **Night Over Water** - K Follett (Pan £4.99)

...

20th June 2018

It strikes me that the NHS has no leadership and plenty of money while the MOD has plenty of fine leaders but no money. There is a simple solution here - surely?

...

1st August 2015

Blue Moon on Friday, *Daily Telegraph's* red face on Saturday. (Today's DT page 2) Hardly a blue moon!

. . .

Published

30th October 2018

SIR – I am glad the soldier in the Duke of Lancaster Regiment, featured in your photograph (October 29), had a wood to fight in for his training.

I have, over the years, been obliged to take part in JEWTs – jungle exercises without trees – and even DEWDs (desert exercises without dunes). Others included, memorably, a NEWD – night exercise without darkness – during which, as second lieutenants under training, we were required to transit Woodbury Common's numerous obstacles wearing blindfolds.

The TEWT – tactical exercise without troops – is well-known to military officers while, sadly, our maritime forces seem to be heading for a series of NEWS, or naval exercises without ships. I once conducted a SLEWP, appropriately named for the yacht club in which I was lecturing. When the projector broke during the second of 50 slides I was forced to continue with a slide show extravaganza without pictures.

. . .

11th January 2024

Now that Fujitsu's failings have been exposed it is high time the government turned its attention to Capita for failing to recruit for the armed forces.

…

19th March 2019

[Expressing horror at the vulgar sculpture, called The Messenger, that suddenly appeared outside Plymouth's Theatre Royal.]

It is a great pity that The Messenger's journey did not end at the bottom of Plymouth Sound during its journey by sea. When I mentioned to my sister, who works at the Theatre Royal outside which it now stands (or crouches), that the statue reminded me of someone having difficulty going to the loo she replied:

Three years ago, at supper, I was sitting next to the architect responsible for the installation when I pointed out to him that (in the original mock-ups) when it rained, the water would run down between her (then) pronounced buttocks, and make it look like as though she was peeing! He was appalled - why had no one noticed before he wondered. After that adjustments were made.

Not enough adjustments, in my (clearly philistine!) view.

The Messenger outside Plymouth's Theatre Royal

…

16th October2019

[Comments about Maltese driving habits.]

Charles Moore reminds us the Maltese (*pace* the Cypriots) alone among their Mediterranean neighbours, drive on the left. My life-long love affair with Malta, Gozo and their wonderfully laid-back inhabitants began in the 1950s when my family lived on the main island. Discussions would occasionally turn to thoughts of whether or not a swop to right-hand driving could ever be considered. The accepted views were, first, that any change from left to right would make no difference to the then driving habits and, secondly, driving would, anyway, only take place on the sunny side of the street. Times may have changed but…!

…

22nd February 2019

[Ms Begum of ISIS had had her British nationality revoked yet she was married to a Dutchman.]

Surely The Netherlands has a duty of care for the wife and son of one of its citizens, or did the Dutch parliament beat us to it by removing Shamima Begum's husband's nationality even earlier?

…

Published

13th November 2020

[Following a discussion on best-before dates.]

SIR – A few years ago, Peter Cameron, a Royal Marines helicopter pilot, suffered serious injuries on my boat.

The haemorrhaging leg wound required a tourniquet and, in the dark, we applied a government-issued "first field dressing".

Once he had been lifted ashore by the coastguard, we inspected the packaging: the dressing was dated 1944. I am glad to report that Peter survived.

Conversation between the yacht and the 999 operator:

Yacht: *We have the haemorrhage under control.*

999 operator: *Are you medically qualified?*

Yacht: *No but between the four of us we have about 100 years of experience with gunshot wounds.*

999 operator: *GUNSHOT WOUNDS! GUNSHOT WOUNDS! You'll need the police!*

…

16th March 2020

[Suggestion that the TV licence be temporarily cancelled for those over 70 during the during the plague.]

I cannot think of a more appropriate time to cancel TV licences for those over 70 – and not just for four months.

…

Spring 1955

[An exchange of letters between my godfather and my mother which affected me greatly occurred in the spring of 1955 while I was living with Lieutenant-Colonel Pat Phibbs in his Bristol Channel pilot cutter *Olga*. The following is an extract from my 'haul down report'[1] written for the Royal Yacht Squadron and the Royal Cruising Club.]

Pat's discipline was uncompromising and exacting although he occasionally met his match. When I was just thirteen years old I refused, for some long-forgotten reason, to climb to the truck of the mast to re-reeve the burgee halyards. "Right, pack your kitbag and put it in the dinghy." No second chance. The British Seagull outboard engine took us from the anchorage in St Mawes to Falmouth dockyard railway station where, with a label attached to the collar of my coat for the various guards *en route*, I was despatched, parcel-like, to Waterloo. After at least four changes and well over seven hours I handed my mother a tear-stained note that read, *Darling June, you sent your son to me to be taught seamanship. He has failed! Love, Pat.* I was taken home, fed, bathed and returned to Waterloo the next morning. In Falmouth I handed Pat the same smudged note on the back of which my mother had written. *Darling Pat, I sent my son to you to be taught seamanship. You appear to be failing! Love, June.* I climbed to the truck!

Olga

---

1 See Final Essays.

Summer 2004

[Letter from Pantaenius Yacht Insurance.]

In 2003 I put my then yacht *Black Velvet III* into the French canals at the Somme and slowly motored, in two week stretches, towards Paris. On the 365 day (mid 2004) she was burgled and the gear box ruined. When I asked the insurance company if they would pay for her to be shipped home from 70 miles north-east of Paris their reply was: *No as it is a pity that you do not have your mast and sails with you!*

Black Velvet on the Somme canal

…

14th March 2009

Continuing on its path towards criminalising as many of us as quickly as possible this urban-centric Government has, once again, acted without serious thought to the practicalities of life at sea in a yacht.

Apparently I am shortly to be obliged to notify, 24 hours in advance (I have seen 48 hours quoted elsewhere) and by e-mail, any foreign-going journey I intend making in my yacht, or face a £5,000 fine.

What on earth is going on here? I and my friends go to sea to escape such tyranny. When we leave our moorings in south Devon, we have no idea of our destination. That will depend on the actual weather conditions as soon as we clear the river's mouth and not the predictions of the seldom-precisely-accurate shipping forecasts that only cover the subsequent six hours - not 24. The state of my crews' stomachs, once we have 'slipped the surly bonds of earth' will then be added to the equation. Even so our destination - that almost certainly will not be a 'formal' port or even, heaven forbid, a marina - may alter frequently during the course of the voyage. Decisions will be continually made, re-assessed and changed depending on the many variables and imponderables associated with the sea and wind. This is the freedom and the joy of small-boat cruising.

Putting to sea from Newton Ferrers my vessel is able to cope with any destination which, in an ordinary summer could, on a whim, be as far afield as Iceland or as close as Looe. If, say, we head for the Isles of Scilly and the weather turns bad from the north we could be forced, with no way of informing Westminster, to run downwind to a safe and secluded anchorage on the Biscay coast of France; or we could slug it out to an equally isolated refuge on the south coast of Ireland; by-passing that beautiful and rock-strewn archipelago of the Isles of Scilly. Who knows where we shall end up - until we get there!

Two other practical considerations loom: access to the internet and being erroneously reported as overdue. The government presumes that small vessels have an internet connection for 24 hours a day but few have such devices and, those that do, find a 24 hour connection unusual. It is, I believe, also very expensive. Without internet and since the lamentable removal of the coast radio stations, with their range far in excess of a mobile telephone (which not all of us take to sea either I am glad to say) we shall have to break our otherwise leisurely progress and make for the expense of a marina berth and an internet café in order to report our new, but not necessarily certain, foreign destination to the totalitarians who now wish to govern our every move, even when at sea. The un-seamanlike requirement to declare, firmly and officially, our destination 24 hours before we even begin to face the elements will lead to a rise in 'overdue' reports, increasing worry to families and unnecessary expenses to the safety services.

Let us continue to do what we have done all our lives: report our safe arrival to our next of kin and the appropriate Coast Guard authorities - *a government agency*. This is unambiguous, factual and fool proof. We all make a very rough plan for our families' peace of mind (and many, on sailing, report their *proposed* passage - whether to a home or foreign destination -

to the relevant Coast Guard station) but for a small sailing vessel to involve central government with its threat of fines to satisfy, it would appear, the far-from-proven argument that it is vital to our country's security, is really not on for British yachtsmen.

At last it might appear that the EU may actually do something good for once! Let us hope so.

…

Published

in the *Daily Telegraph's* book of unpublished letters, *Wake me Up When It's All Over.*

30th June 2021

Andy Murray has complained that the grass at Wimbledon is too slippery. Next we'll have mariners complaining that the sea is too rough.

…

Published

November 2006

I received recently a letter about my book HMS *Fearless* in which the reader complained of the smell of the pages. Perhaps all books should have the aroma of their subject matter in which case I shall arrange for the reprint to smell of burnt aviation fuel and frying chips!

…

Published

Mid summer 1978

My apiarist wife is surprised to learn that she must now put 'best before dates' on her honey jars. As the Egyptians tell us that honey (and glass) lasts for thousands of years it is a pity that modern tin lids let the side down!

…

Defence

Published

8th January 2019

It has been reported recently that on 4th August 1814 the White House in Washington was 'torched' by the British army. I am happy to correct this misapprehension - it was the Royal Marines who, despite the best efforts of the United States Marine Corp, entered the city to set fire to the Capitol and the White House.

...

Published

27th March 1997

[Following a rather uneducated letter suggesting that the SAS were employed world-wide with British Army Training Teams and especially in the Oman.]

Drag up a sandbag, Michael Smith (*Big Business For Officers of Fortune - 27 March*) and let me swing the lamp for a moment.

I cannot speak for the seventies - nor for those areas outside the Oman in the sixties - but it is a common fault to accept that all BATTs (British Army Training Teams) throughout the world consisted solely of SAS members and, indeed, that that Regiment was totally responsible for eventual victory in Dhofar (as is often implied) although they certainly played their part there.

Along with a number of other officers and SNCOs from the Royal Marines and Army I was 'on loan' (a mercenary?) from the Royal Marines to the Sultan of Muscat's Army between 1966 and 1968. Thankfully, none of us were members of the SAS nor of a BATT (I never heard the expression until well into the seventies)) and although some were involved in training most were in operational command at all levels from Commander of the Armed Forces to platoon commander.

I was privileged to command a reconnaissance platoon and a rifle company of Omani and Baluchi soldiers in the Dhofar war against a communist-inspired uprising against the then Sultan, Said bin Taimur, long before any SAS became involved. Nor was Britain the only country to supply 'loan soldiers' for on the 11th January 1968 and after three skirmishes with the enemy during which we lost two dead and four wounded we discovered the enemy had lost twenty wounded and twelve killed, among whom was a Chinese 'adviser' - perhaps a member of CATTs?

...

14th January 2020

[Following Sultan Qaboos's obituary that implied that the SAS had won the Dhofar war.]

I regret that your obituary of Sultan Qaboos bin Said does his armed forces a grave disservice – if not a severe insult. (Letters January 14)

It is stated that 'between 1970 and 1975 the SAS and assorted British advisers waged a secret war in Dhofar'. This, most emphatically, is not correct. The war had been waged, savagely and not entirely successfully, since 1965 by poorly equipped but hugely enthusiastic units of the Sultan's Armed Forces (SAF): the Muscat, Northern Frontier and Desert regiments supported by the Oman Gendarmerie, the Sultan of Oman's Air Force and the navy's one motorised dhow all commanded and trained by British contract and seconded personnel. With the arrival of Sultan Qaboos (almost coinciding with the first exports of oil) money was at last available for proper uniforms, up-dated field medicine, modern weapons and aircraft plus the formation of artillery and cavalry regiments and the beginnings of a modern navy. Thus the army's fortunes could slowly be reversed with the help, too, of Iranian and Jordanian forces.

Yes, the SAS played their part from 1970 onwards with a hearts and minds campaign plus the recruiting of ex- enemy tribesmen into the SAF but these notably-volatile *firqat* were actually commanded by a remarkable British contract officer and Arabist, lately from a highland regiment.

Those of us who served in the Dhofar War were mightily relieved to have done so before the arrival of the SAS who thought they would soon thrash what they insultingly called a collection of 'ragheads', but whose initial contacts with the *adoo*[2] were little short of disastrous.

If anyone should want the balanced truth of how that war was won they could do no better than ignore the books written by retired SAS officers and instead study the seminal work by Major-General John Akehurst called, correctly, *We Won a War.*

Lately of the Oman's Northern Frontier and Desert Regiments.

2 Enemy.

Published

8th October 2010

[Following an article questioning the need for amphibious forces.]

Since 1945, British forces have been on active service in Korea, Malaya, Hong Kong, Cyprus, Suez, Kuwait, Aden, Borneo, Brunei, East Africa, South Georgia, the Falklands, Lebanon, Sierra Leone, Kosovo, Iraq, the Congo, Belize, Northern Ireland and Afghanistan. All but one of these campaigns (I have not included worldwide commitments to day to day anti-drug and piracy operations) included Royal Marines Commandos who were often landed, with surprise, from the sea as the Army was either too stretched to cope or, often, unable to gain that first vital foothold that only a force projected from over the horizon can hope to achieve in significant - instant - strength. The opening stages of the current Afghan campaign were launched from an amphibious task force operating in the Gulf.

Significantly, most of these campaigns were counter-insurgency and not state-on-state - which the generals seem to think is the only war in which the Royal Navy will play any significant part - and yet the fleet was always there with its incomparable amphibious and special forces backed up by sea-based, fixed- and rotary-wing aircraft plus, vitally, naval gunfire.

Additionally the Royal Fleet Auxiliary and civilian ships, protected by the fleet, tended to - and will continue to - supply the 95 per cent of all *materiel* needed by land forces. Nor must we forget the role played solely by naval forces in numerous humanitarian and disaster relief operations in all hemispheres.

The current amphibious fleet is paid for, balanced, easily tailored for most foreseeable eventualities and needs no 'host-nation' support: an increasingly un-likely luxury. Emasculating it to one fixed-wing carrier, converted to carry Royal Marines, protected by just 12 available escorts, most of whom will be in refit or deployed on other duties - as your Defence Correspondent seems to suggest is the wish of the Admiralty Board - is lunacy and certainly unworkable. I pray - for the country's sake - that your reporter is incorrect.

We should remember that prior to the Falklands Task Force being despatched it was only the Chief of Naval Staff who offered to rescue the situation. Initially the army and air force Chiefs of Staff refused to be involved in what they thought would be a bloody nose for the Royal Navy; but then we also had a naval officer as Chief of Defence Staff. Now the generals seem to think they can fight with no Royal Navy support: well, we shall see, and I bet they will be as wrong now as the admirals were right in 1982!

Editor *Jane's Amphibious and Special Forces* 1997 to 2013.

...

15th September 2017

[Following an MOD announcement on further defence cuts.]

Stand by for the usual stream of platitudes which will be uttered by the Secretary of State for Defence from his ivory tower of denial; also known as the Ministry of Defeat.

...

Published

in the *Western Morning News* on 13th January 2024

6th January 2024

[Reports that the two amphibious assault ships are to be placed in permanent maintenance so that their crews can man other ships.]

I wonder if the Secretary of State for Defence is aware that Britain's amphibious forces are trained and equipped for very much more than storming beaches, D Day-style. Most future campaigns and likely areas of disaster relief will still require landings across beaches or through damaged ports to establish that first vital foothold. Only the Royal Navy's dwindling amphibious forces can do just that while air-transported troops need friendly airspace and an undamaged or un-defended runway before they can begin to play their part.

The current Royal Fleet Auxiliaries, with other surface warships, can provide much invaluable practical help and sustenance, but none can transport ashore equipment such as heavy-lift vehicles for the onward movement of aide and the rebuilding of basic facilities - including air strips. As has been shown, time and time again, only HMSs *Albion* and *Bulwark* (and their forebears, *Fearless* and *Intrepid*) with their shallow-draft landing craft and hovercraft - the latter ideal for river work or in an area strewn with debris - plus their helicopters and embarked military force can be of any practical and lasting value in the initial stages of war or natural disaster. These ships' integrated Amphibious Beach Units, with their ability to repair damaged ports, are unique among the British armed forces. Now, if the signs from Whitehall are to be believed, these two remarkable 'amphibious assault ships', the key to so many successful operations in peace and war since 1965, are to be left in permanent reserve and we know what that means: they will never see blue water again.

It is not just the ships that will be lost under the MOD's cost saving plans but, with them, the possibility of conducting any form of entry or exit across hostile or damaged shores in time of conflict or, perhaps of more importance, disaster relief.

...

Published

for the first time in the *Daily Telegraph*!

31st March 2006

SIR - Most future campaigns and likely areas of disaster relief might still require landing across beaches or through damaged ports.

While the current Royal Fleet Auxiliaries and other surface warships can provide much invaluable help, none can lift ashore equipment such as heavy-lift transport for the onward movement of aid. Only HMS Albion and HMS Bulwark, with their shallow-draft landing craft and hovercraft - the latter ideal for river work or in areas strewn with debris - can be of any practical and lasting value. Their Amphibious Beach Units, with their ability to build or rebuild beach landing sites or port facilities, are unique in the British Armed Forces.

It is not just the ships that will be lost under these costing-cutting plans but, with them, the possibility of conducting any form of entry or exit across hostile or damaged shores.

Lt-Col Ewen Southby-Tailyour RM
Ermington, Devon

...

Published

for the second time in the Daily Telegraph!

3rd November 2017

[Following yet another suggestion that the United Kingdom no longer needs an amphibious capability.]

Most future campaigns and likely areas of disaster relief might still require landing across beaches or through damaged ports.

While the current Royal Fleet Auxiliaries and other surface warships can provide much invaluable help, none can transport ashore equipment such as heavy-lift vehicles for the onward movement of aid. Only HMS *Albion* and HMS *Bulwark*, with their shallow-draft landing craft and hovercraft - the latter ideal for river work or an area strewn with debris- can be of any practical and lasting value. The Amphibious Beach Units, with their ability to build or rebuild beach landing sites or port facilities, are unique in the British Armed Forces.

It is not just the ships that will be lost under these cost cutting plans but, with them, the possibility of conducting any form of entry or exit across hostile or damaged shores.

HMS Albion

...

Published

20th January 2020

[Various discussions on the future Captain General of the Royal Marines following Prince Harry's 'retirement'. A few days before this letter was published it had been speculated that Princess Anne could become the next Captain General of the Royal Marines - which is actually what we all wanted but felt that she might have been too busy. Sitting next to the Princess Royal at a Trinity House dinner one month after this letter was published she commented in her introduction to my speech that I was 'an inveterate writer of letters to the *Daily Telegraph*!']

HRH and ES-T at the Trinity House dinner

I know it is nothing to do with a retired Royal Marines officer so I hope I will be excused if I suggest two names as our possible Captain General following the 'retirement' of Prince Harry.

On the assumption that the 'rules' do not forbid a foreigner from the post I would like to have suggested King Harald V of Norway as he is already an Honorary Colonel in our Corps… but he was born in 1937.

My second suggestion is King Willem-Alexander of the Netherlands, born in 1967. Bearing in mind the very close working association that the Royal Marines have with the Royal Netherlands Marine Corps and that King Willem-Alexander was not only an officer in the Royal Netherlands Navy, but is an avid cross-country skier and qualified pilot, I would have thought he would be a pretty good and most welcome choice.

...

Published

15th August 2007

[This followed a complaint that those serving in Helmand province of Afghanistan were not being awarded a separate campaign medal.]

In 1982, the South Atlantic Medal was awarded to all those who took part in Operation Corporate. Those involved - how do I put this tactfully? - in the real fighting were, additionally, awarded a 'rosette'. What's the difference in Afghanistan?

...

Essay Published
in the *Marine Quarterly*

5th March 2012

[No reply received.]

The Rt Hon, David Cameron PC,

To coincide with the 30th anniversary of the Argentine invasion of South Georgia and the Falkland Islands I enclose an essay (not attached here) discussing the present conundrum as I see it. I know it is long but it is an important subject.

I begin by outlining the background to the present situation. I then comment on Mrs Kirchner's problems. Following that I talk about the Falklands prior to 1982. Then I discuss and compare the relative military situations in Argentina and the United Kingdom in 1982 and 2012.

Finally, after highlighting the strengths and weaknesses on both sides I suggest a possible operation by Argentina to re-take the islands culminating in Britain's inability to react.

I have sent a copy to the Editor of the *Daily Telegraph* but have not asked for it to be published: unless he specifically requests. The original was written for *Marine Quarterly* and will be published in June.

I regret that neither you, your two Secretaries of State for Defence nor your various armed forces advisors come out of it well. (Nor do earlier administrations of both persuasions.) Frankly, you all listen far too closely to the single-service views of the Royal Air Force.

...

18th April 2021

[HRH Prince Philip's funeral coverage.]

It much saddens us Royal Marines, past and present, let alone those members of the bearer party, that the precision and attention to detail shown by the armed forces yesterday at the funeral of HRH Prince Philip,

Duke of Edinburgh is in marked contrast to your inaccurate reporting of events.

The caption to the double page photograph on pages 7 and 8 erroneously states that the 1st Battalion the Grenadier Guards carried the coffin into St George's Chapel. This most difficult and delicate of all the events that day was conducted, impeccably, by eight senior non-commissioned officers, one regimental sergeant major and one captain of the Royal Marines. This was in accordance with the Duke's wishes – our Captain General since 1953. This unforgivable error was even compounded in your Editorial. On all days this was one when attention to accuracy should have been paramount.

For the sake of historical facts you really must print a large, unambiguous correction.

...

19th April 2021

[More on the same subject. As the result of an inexcusable and unpardonable error in yesterday's *Sunday Telegraph* I wrote, in part, the following:]

Chris Evans Esq.,

Allister Heath Esq.,

It much saddens us Royal Marines, past and present, let alone those members of the bearer party, that the precision and attention to detail shown by the armed forces yesterday at the funeral of His Royal Highness Prince Philip, Duke of Edinburgh is in marked contrast to your inaccurate reporting of events.

The caption to the double page photograph on pages 8 and 9 erroneously states that the 1st Battalion the Grenadier Guards carried the duke's coffin into St George's Chapel. This most difficult and delicate of all the events that day was conducted, impeccably, by eight senior non-commissioned officers, one regimental sergeant major and one captain of the Royal Marines. This was in accordance with the Duke's wishes – our Captain General since 1953.

This unforgivable error in reporting was, inexplicably, even repeated in your Editorial. Of all days this was one when attention to accuracy should have been paramount - but, instead, you have let history down.

I know that your two newspapers are separate but as you are both from the same stable I had hoped that today's *Daily Telegraph* might have found some way of rectifying this; perhaps simply by publishing my letter.

Furthermore, this morning I have had the opportunity of reading in detail, the *Sunday Telegraph's* eight page, black-edged supplement. Despite the front page showing the Royal Marine's' bearer party leading the royal procession nowhere inside does the name Royal Marines exist – indeed the Royal Navy is not mentioned either. Nor, for that matter is the Royal Air Force although most army regiments get a mention.

Considering that the Royal Marines bearer party had - by far - the most difficult, demanding, delicate and public part to play (and immediately in front of the Royal Family) their omission is inexcusable. Is it too much to hope that sometime this week - perhaps next Sunday, although that would be leaving it too late - this disgraceful blunder can be corrected, alongside a prominent apology? Frankly, not to do so would be nothing short of a disgrace.

You might care, too, to mention by name the ten members of the Royal Marines bearer party who had the greatest honour of all throughout the whole proceedings

...

Published

1st May 2018

[Referring to an article written for the *Times* by Major Duncan Christie-Miller, RM.]

SIR – Our Royal Marines commando training was once – famously and correctly – encapsulated in an article titled: "You can't get hard in a soft bed".

...

30th March 2011

[The ineffective use of the RAF in Libya.]

The RAF has sent *Typhoons* and *Tornados* (only three of the nine made it all the way) via expensive airborne re-fuelling, to an Italian air base. This 'forward airfield' was still far enough away from their eventual target for these aircraft to require yet more airborne refuelling before destroying, by last weekend's count, only four main battle tanks and five armoured vehicles. What an extraordinary waste of fuel, airframe, engine and pilot hours.

Attacking ground targets is a task perfectly suited to the Royal Marine and Royal Navy pilots of 847 Naval Air Squadron with their anti-tank helicopters operating from an amphibious ship or aircraft carrier lying twelve and a half miles offshore.

Add to that the unarguable fact that their time on target would be far greater than that of the RAF's aircraft while their ability to conduct many missions per day, totalling a fraction of the cost of just one RAF mission, would be unarguable. The advantage of 'loitering' would provide complete flexibility and avoid -as happened recently over Libya -the last minute abortion of a mission by aircraft that had flown all the way from the United Kingdom.

Is this not, too, a task for which the Army Air Corps' *Apache* was largely procured? Nor should we forget the proven ability of the Fleet Arm Arm's

Harriers to conduct precision bombing operations against vehicles moving fast through deep, steep-sided mountain valleys: terrain unsuitable for faster aircraft.

...

11th April 2011

[The same subject.]

The RAF staff have always had their sights on the Commando Helicopter Force. Politicians, gullible to RAF cant, must be made to understand clearly that the Royal Navy and Royal Marines pilots are not only – and vitally – close friends and colleagues of those they support but, crucially, they understand the ground battle while their squadrons are permanently intertwined in the Commando Brigade's Order of Battle. These three paramount aspects of the CHF cannot be cast aside at the jealous whim of the Air Marshalls. This is not inter-service rivalry but sheer common sense. Some will remember when, in a RAF staff paper to prove that they were able to cover targets that in practice they could not, Australia was 'moved' north by some hundreds of miles: the RAF staff are now up to the same trick with Cyprus. Politicians must see through these un-subtle and deceitful manoeuvrings.

...

13th April 2011

Many fail to understand why the government and the RAF are undertaking a massively non-cost-effective operation simply to engage elderly armoured vehicles. The RAF, after just a few weeks, now admits it cannot continue this task as their pilots are untrained! Surely this is a role for the Army Air Corp's *Apache* helicopters and was a task perfectly suited to the pilots of 847 Naval Air Squadron operating from an amphibious ship close in shore -and not off Scotland's coast nor that of Italy! The *Harrier* was pretty good - and cheap - at it too.

...

20th April 2011

[Yet more on the same subject.]

Graham Butler (Letters April 20) highlights what many have appreciated since long before the Libyan crisis. There are aircraft designed specifically for engaging ground targets in such a small-scale conflict where air-superiority exists. They are the Fleet Air Arm's *Harriers* and the Army Air Corps' *Apache*. Additionally, until it was re-configured, the Royal Marines and Royal Navy pilots of 847 Naval Air Squadron operated, and still could, anti-tank helicopters: all flying off an amphibious vessel close in shore, and not off Scotland's coast nor even that of Italy.

These ship-based aircraft are capable of delivering multiple anti-armour ordnance and of strafing suitable targets: they would, too, have time to be selective.

It would be sensible to return to those militarily- and economically-viable days!

...

14th May 2019

[The Chief of the Defence Staff's blinkered view comes under attack.]

Lord Houghton's naïve misunderstanding of the long-term, strategic, tri-service and diplomatic value of the country's two aircraft carriers almost outclasses Lord Stirrup's equally xenophobic and premature scrapping of the *Harriers* (below) and the invaluable and war-proven carriers from which they flew.

...

14th February 2023

I agree wholeheartedly with Squadron Leader David Lott about the superb Harrier as an air defence and ground attack aircraft and I lament, with him, their premature disposal to the US Marine Corps. Sadly, though, it was a member of his own service, Marshall of the Royal Air Force Lord Stirrup who, when Chief of the Defence staff between 2006 to 2010, oversaw this indefensible step. They could indeed be the near-perfect answer to Ukraine's air defence. Perhaps the USMC should take note!

...

Apology

received from the obituary writer.

5th December 2023

[The obituary writer (whom I know) had not done his research thoroughly!]

In his otherwise wholesome and well-deserved tribute to Commander Andy Johnson your naval obituary writer is not quite accurate. He states that HMS *Onyx's* achievements had to wait until, at the earliest, 2015 to be made public. My book, *Exocet Falklands*, was published in 2014 when, for the first time, Operation Kettledrum was mentioned in close detail, including the reasons for its cancellation, which were not quite as described.

Up to 2014 no one outside those that took part knew of the operation and so it was with some considerable reluctance that the then CO SBS allowed me to mention it. I also describe the damage to the torpedo tube shutters and the eventual removal of the torpedo - including a photograph that had not been released before publication.

As an aside, and as described in *Exocet Falklands*, there were just seven, not 12, Royal Marines embarked in the submarine, six for the operation itself together with the SBS's operations officer.

Due to numerous reasons such as the 20 nautical miles approach by rubber dinghy, the extreme hydrographic conditions and the vast length of the escape route to a neutral country, let alone the fact that there never had been Exocet-carrying Super Étendard bombers based at Puerto

Deseado, there is no doubt at all that the operation would have failed with the loss of six men.

Operation Kettledrum had been dreamt up in Northwood over three weeks earlier by staff officers with, rather obviously, no up-to-date intelligence. Thankfully, almost at the last moment, it was cancelled by those on the spot who had more important operations to plan.

...

19th July 1993

[Complaint about the appalling behaviour within Defence Procurement that led to collapse of one of the United Kingdom's very best shipbuilders, Swan Hunters - with whom I had worked.]

Jonathan Aitken, Esq., MP Minister of State for Defence Procurement.

Once the collapse of Swan Hunters is confirmed there will be no competition for the design and build of the two new assault ships, announced by Mister Rifkind last week. Without competitors how can the government follow its own policy of competitive tendering?

In 1993's November/December issue of *Navy International* under the title *Amphibious Warfare, a British Résumé*[3] I explained that there were only two companies capable of building ships of the size of a *Fearless* replacement.

With today's announcement that Swan Hunters have not been awarded the *Sir Bedivere*refit contract, it is now almost certain that they will not survive and we will be left with just one capable yard. You were well aware of the penalties to Swans if they were unsuccessful with this bid and while that decision may have been the correct one in the short-term, you must also have been aware of the penalties to the future of amphibious warfare of procuring a major amphibious ship from a one company (VSEL)with, effectively now, a monopoly for ships of this size.

On this evening's BBC PM programme you stated that sentiment could play no part in defence contracts; maybe not, but the defence of our country should be based on longer term projects, than merely the securing of one cheap LSL refit.

---

3 See the penultimate essay in the final section.

If the declared policy of competitive tendering is considered to be the best way to get not only get value for money, but to meet the Staff Requirement (Sea), then the desire to offer the work to the cheapest tenderer should have taken second place to the more important business of keeping Swan Hunters alive. This would have ensured that the government's preferred procurement route was maintained for the benefit of the men who would have to serve and fight in the new ships: there would have been nothing sentimental about that.

Incidentally, a wise old gentleman in the Procurement Executive told me that it was, more often than not, folly to opt for the cheapest bid, even if it met the Naval Staff Requirement (as it was then known), for his experience showed that all ships have, in general, a finite price and anyone significantly below the norm had achieved their figures by imaginative, accounting and would always have to review their costs once the contract had been won and was too late to stop. VSEL, with HMS *Ocean* and British Aerospace with the LPD basic design study are prime, recent and relevant examples.

The VSEL ship will almost certainly end up costing more than Swans version (and it was never quite as good a design as first presented) and the British Aerospace project has run over budget, with a consequent cutting of other projects.

The direct result of your decision is that with no competition the amphibious forces are in danger of receiving second-best. In much the same way as amphibious troops are treated by the downgrading of the LPH: ostensibly to save money, but in practice (and by an underhand method) to get the same size chip for less. This was achieved by reducing design capacity on paper (and therefore on the costing sheet), yet still requiring the original numbers of embarked force to be carried, now at 'overload'. In effect they are carried for free which must please the Treasury, but will certainly not impress the long-suffering but ever patient men.

The fact that the new LPH's is actually designed to carry 3/8ths of its planned military force at overload, to save this money, seems not to matter to those who will not have to suffer the discomfort (not to say the insult and indignity) well into the 21st century. These facts were highlighted by me in *Navy International.*

Forgetting the strange process by which VSEL did win the contract for HMS *Ocean*, where does this latest decision leave the government's competitive tendering policy and is it not about time that the arguments and points raised in *Navy International* received serious thought.

On behalf of all those serving senior officers who cannot speak, but whose views I know well, they asked you to think again about allowing Swan Hunters to go by default. The news that the amphibious forces are to get their two badly needed assault ships is of course excellent but, to refer to the subtitle of my magazine article, why spoil this vital adjunct to our defence policy for a happorth of tar: at least stave off the final execution (if it has to come to that, eventually) one of Britain's finest designers and builders of *inter alia*, large ships (and the only yard capable of giving VSEL competition) until Swans have had a chance to bid.

I have no axe to grind *vis-á-vis* the two shipyards. I have worked very happily with both on various projects and hope to continue doing so-nor do I mind who is awarded the contract for the assault ships, providing that it is bid for in a fair and competitive manner.

I do, though, have a serious concern of the effectiveness of the equipment supplied to our amphibious forces.

Answered

on 5 August on behalf of the Minister of State by the then Director General Surface Ships (DGSS) in a long and typical example of Whitehall obfuscation.

There was, most empathetically, nothing fair (as the DGSS wrote) about the manner in which the LPH (HMS *Ocean*) was removed from Swan Hunters (who had been told they had won the contract) the night before the decision was announced and offered to VSEL - who by some slight of financial hand had managed- overnight to reduce their costs by £40M.

It is astounding that civil servants in the MOD can see no further than their own noses and assume that no one else is capable of seeing the real truth!

HMS Ocean

...

28th March 2018

Captain Robert Pedre, Royal Navy, HMS *Ocean*,

I was honoured to be invited to the Decommissioning Ceremony of HMS *Ocean* yesterday in the presence of Her Majesty and thank you very much indeed for the invitation.

For my last four years in the Royal Marines (1988 - 1992) I was on the design teams at Foxhill, Bath, for the LPH and LPD's helping to write the military aspects of the Procurement Specifications and then advising those shipyards that submitted their tenders for the work. Later I was a member of the teams that assessed the designs before helping the Procurement Executive make their definitive decisions. A most satisfying end to my career that had been spent mostly in amphibious work - beginning with HMS *Anzio* in the Persian Gulf in 1963. It is, though, sad that in the few short years since those exciting days I was to witness the premature end of such a fine ship.

Nevertheless, yesterday was a glorious occasion enhanced by what I thought was the quite superb drill of your Royal Guard of Honour, yours and Her Majesty's evocative speeches and, on a more personal level, the superbly-delicious buffet lunch in the hangar and the meeting of many old friends. All in all a marvellous day and I thank you most sincerely for allowing me to be part of it.

...

Unknown date

[Comment on the totally inappropriate uniform of the Chief of the Defence Staff at a Downing Street meeting.]

Putting aside for a moment the eminently sensible - if rather late - decision to bring the Armed Forces into play with their unsurpassed experience in crisis management, why on earth does the Chief of the Defence Staff have to appear as though he was a recruit that had just climbed out of a slit trench on Salisbury Plain?

Throughout the Falkland's campaign Ian MacDonald, during his nightly televised briefings, was accompanied by Lieutenant-Colonel (then) Tim Donkin in the day-dress uniform of the Royal Marines. This was the appropriate rig and, being smart and clean, brought the correct amount of gravitas to the solemnity of the occasion. This cannot be said of an officer appearing, laughably, in his you-cannot-see-me suit and a green T-shirt.

...

3rd April 2017

[Cutting of front-line forces instead of the 'tail'.]

I have never understood the incomprehensible logic that requires successive Secretaries of State for Defence to emasculate those organizations closest to the enemy. Common sense and military expediency suggest that cuts should fall on those furthest from the action: there is still fat in the defence industry so why cut the muscle. With Spanish sabres rattling does the government not remember the proposed scrapping of HMSs *Endurance*, *Fearless* and *Intrepid* - plus the then carriers - and the consequences 35 years ago?

Additionally, cuts that effect the country's fighting ability should not be a single-service exercise for, in this case, the First Sea Lord alone to decide: the loss of a third of the only Royal Marine commando brigade is not a national issue, it is, through NATO, an international one.

If aircraft for the new carriers are delayed - as seem probable - then these ships will have to revert to their secondary role as 'commando carriers' (or have no role at all) but without a balanced amphibious commando brigade to embark they, too will become largely impotent.

Can Michael Fallon really risk this enviable, world-wide reputation for the sake of 400 sailors?

...

4th November 2019

[Ridiculous proposal to change the ranks and uniforms of Royal Marines officers to those of the Royal Navy but not those of the marines themselves!]

I read of rumours that consideration might be given to change the ranks of Royal Marines from those of the army to those of the Royal Navy. I hope those in the Ministry of Defence and the Admiralty, responsible for such fundamental matters, will remember that for 355 years we have been, and remain, 'sea-soldiers' and not 'land-sailors'.

...

Unknown date

[Fallon wished he had been on board for the patrol!]

If Sir Michael Fallon is unable to keep his hands of a woman for five minutes in a public studio what hope for his female shipmates had he been submerged in HMS *Vigilant* for three months.

...

19th August 2020

[The Defence Secretary, Williamson, was publically described as behaving in a similar fashion to Private Pyke in Dad's Army.]

If you send a boy to do a man's job, what can you expect?

...

Published

18th July 2023

The armed forces are to receive a 5% pay rise - inevitably, the lowest of all public sector employees. Why? Simply because the government is, as expected and as always, taking advantage of our inability to strike.

This is a disgrace for a service that is on call 24 hours a day not only for life-threatening operations to protect the nation's security and interests at home and overseas but, shamefully, one that is also required to stand in when those with higher salaries and pay rises, down tools.

This will not help a dipping recruitment and retention rate and thus will - along with the illogical reduction in numbers - further reduce our ability to meet our commitments. In more honourable days senior officers and ministers would resign in protest but now they are just resigned to this continuing injustice.

...

24th April 2010

Following Con Coughlin's rather strange - not to say inaccurate - comments about the Royal Navy (*Britain needs the Navy to provide firepower – not a ferry service*) I wonder if you would be interested in publishing the attached (*Boots on the Ground*, below) that I wrote for, and that was published, in *Warship* and repeated in the *Globe & Laurel.*

As not many in the naval service recognise much in Coughlin's piece we feel that a balanced riposte - rather than a necessarily short letter - to a wider readership than hitherto will go some way towards redressing our very genuine concerns. We hope you think so too!

…

Published

in the *Globe and Laurel*

BOOTS ON THE GROUND - COURTESY OF THE ROYAL NAVY

The recent spats - true or imagined by the press - between the Chiefs of Staff are unfortunate. The desire to manipulate the media and politicians in advance of the promised Defence Review is understandable yet it is not the business of individuals to second-guess future threats in order to influence strategies, budgets, capabilities and force levels to their advantage.

Many in, or retired from, the naval service are concerned with the direction in which some of this jostling for the lion's share is heading. Army-supporting, 'defence' correspondents believe that the modern Royal Navy has a role to play but only in state-on-state campaigns and not the expected counter-insurgency operations: this is a Jutland or Trafalgar complex. No one can accurately assess the style of future warfare in this continuing, uncertain era, yet this very uncertainty allows some to suggest that the Royal Navy should be cut.

One journalist argues that Britain must emulate states like Canada, Australia 'and others' who are, at the expense of their naval forces, considering an increase in the size of their infantry by 20 per cent. Yet, unlike the United Kingdom - and, to a lesser extent, Australia - most of these 'other countries' do not have international responsibilities for which they might expect, occasionally, to act independently with a balance of sea, land and air forces.

More often these 'other countries' act as force-multipliers through supplying troops and little else to a coalition. Unable to 'go it alone', this is a useful contribution to the overall effort. Clearly unknown to the journalist - and paradoxically - these two countries, plus an increasing number of others, while planning to increase their infantry, are actually boosting their naval forces by procuring large combat-support ships with helicopter spots, landing craft and docks.

What is certain is that the United Kingdom will, regardless of the nature of future conflicts, require substantial naval and amphibious forces to conduct unforeseen operations in pursuit of foreign policies; to safeguard our fishing and mining rights and to meet a myriad of extant, overseas obligations. The safeguarding of our trading routes alone, both in home waters and in the world's maritime choke points, is a separate subject and one that would not include too many mentions of either the army or the air force.

It may not be war-fighting but only naval forces can bring near-instant help in time of natural disasters or when British nationals - under armed threat - need evacuating.

To support these unequivocal views we must look back over six decades. Since 1945, British forces have been involved in Korea, Malaya, Hong Kong, Cyprus, Suez, Kuwait, Aden, Oman, Borneo, Brunei, East Africa, South Georgia, the Falklands, Southern Thule, Sierra Leone, Bosnia, Kosovo, Iraq, south-east Turkey, Honduras, Nicaragua, the Congo, Belize, Northern Ireland and Afghanistan. All these campaigns - tellingly, most of them were counter-insurgency and not state-on-state -included Royal Marines' Commando Forces, often landed with surprise from the sea when the army was either too stretched to cope or, sometimes, unable to gain that first vital foothold that only a force projected from over the horizon can hope to achieve in significant strength.

In most conflicts (some exclusively so) the Royal Navy was deeply involved with its incomparable special and amphibious forces backed-up by sea-based fixed- and rotary-wing aircraft plus naval gunfire. Additionally the Royal Fleet Auxiliary and civilian ships, protected by the fleet from surface (including piracy), sub-surface (mines and submarines) and air threats, tended to (and will continue to) supply 95 per cent of all *materiel* that has to travel by sea. Ignore this fact and it will not matter a jot how many 'boots' are on the ground nor whether they are facing an international crisis or a local uprising.

The Royal Navy enjoys an added advantage over the other services; the ability to provide an influential, balanced, co-ordinated, sea, ground and air deterrent that operates in neutral waters and air space while able, at will, to advance or retire over hundreds of miles in any twenty-four hour period. No other force, regardless of size, can exert such benign - or, if necessary, malign - pressure. A single vessel can, too, make a difference. In 1977 one submarine effectively pre-empted a possible invasion of the Falklands: five years on, another single boat prevented further naval action.

Senior officers might, too, reflect that, for a quarter of all Afghanistan's *Herrick* operations, the naval service deploys more personnel into theatre than the army. Further reflection will show that an undeniable bonus comes with this naval force. Its members, of all ranks - whether their background is the sea, the ground, the air, logistics or medical - have spent much of their professional lives working alongside each other.

Most army brigades in Helmand - *pace* 16 Air Assault Brigade - can make no such boast and to prove the point elsewhere, in 1982 a hastily cobbled together brigade with no organic logistic support nor transport, caused untold problems for itself and the Royal Fleet Auxiliary.

Nor should we forget that, prior to the Falklands Task Force being despatched, it was only the Chief of Naval Staff who was determined to rescue the situation. The other Chiefs did not wish to be involved in what they were convinced would be a bloody nose for the Royal Navy. Thankfully, for the Islanders and our own national pride, the Chief of Defence Staff was also an admiral. It is now ironical that the generals think they can operate - as they nearly forced the Royal Navy to do in 1982 - with reduced support from the other services: we shall see, and I bet they will be as wrong then as the admirals were right - and courageous - prior to *Operation Corporate*!

We need more infantry in the field - we always need extra sappers - but we also need helicopter spots at sea so that those 'boots' (marines and army) with their supporting arms can be delivered safely and timely when conditions - politically, geographically and tactically - are not conducive to 'administrative' landings.

If the army wants more 'boots on the ground' then, of course, a second Royal Marines Commando Brigade - with its attached army units - plus two more LPHs would do the trick nicely! A third carrier and sufficient escorts will also help to keep them there.

...

25th July 2010

[Unfounded and irresponsible rumours that the Royal Marines might be disbanded or transferred to the army.]

May I suggest that until the Strategic Defence and Security Review is delivered your Political Correspondent (James Kirkup) keeps well away from reporting on defence matters (Comment July 24). It is most unlikely and certainly not credible that the 'Navy might lose control of the Royal Marines as the price of its new aircraft carriers' while it is even less convincing that 'to extract a price for the new carriers… the army has drawn up plans to take operational command of the Royal Marines'.

If the object of the exercise is to save money - it should of course be to meet the defence needs of the future - then both of Kirkup's statements are unsustainable. Every maritime country in the world knows that an amphibious force is the key to the future – whether they can afford it or not.

The RM Commando Brigade and the Royal Navy's Amphibious Warfare Squadron are a team: they cannot be split up or would your political correspondent suggest that half the UK's football team joined forces with half the UK's rugby team to play international cricket?

...

28th December 2018

[In answer to the suggestion that 'civilian' craft be used to combat illegal immigration.]

The idea of second-hand patrol boats, in conjunction with light spotter aeroplanes, (Letters December 28) could indeed be a solution that might help stem the flood of illegal immigrants. It would, too, free up both the Royal Navy and the Border Force to confront drugs and arms smugglers, unlawful fishermen, real criminals and the Queen's enemies in general.

However, in both the RN and RAF there is a manpower problem and as the crews of the proposed small vessels and light aircraft need not be trained to service standards may I suggest the reintroduction of the Second World War's remarkably successful Royal Naval Volunteer (Supplementary) Reserve, along with an RAF equivalent.

Prior to 1939 the ranks of the RNV(S)R were mainly drawn from experienced yachtsmen, trawler men and general seaman and were available on an 'as required' basis. These experienced 'amateurs' conducted their own training and received no pay and thus were not a drain on sparse resources yet were irreplaceable once employed (and paid) in manning, for instance, the country's coastal forces. *Plus ça change*?

Sadly for me, so successful was the scheme that the age limit had to be reduced from 39 to 25 and, if implemented now, I do not see it being increased to 78!

...

25th September 2010

[Xenophobic tendencies in the RAF.]

Sadly your report of the SAS being denied parachute training by the RAF, in preference to their own freefall display team, comes as no surprise. In the mid 1980s, when commanding the Royal Marines' 539 Assault Squadron, four of my fast raiding craft that had been on active-service operations near Gibraltar were due to return for further such operations in home waters. On arrival at the airfield for their long-scheduled flight the SNCO in command was told that there was now no room on the aircraft:

inside were two, new, private motor cars being imported into the UK by two RAF officers.

In Plymouth my general demanded to know why my squadron was unable to meet its next operational commitment. Hearing the reason he sought an explanation from the appropriate Air Vice Marshal but the airman's reply was obtuse in the extreme, doing nothing to mitigate the navy's long-standing opinion of the RAF's inwards looking posture.

...

Published

29th October 2018

SIR – I am glad the soldier in the Duke of Lancaster Regiment, featured in your photograph (October 29), had a wood to fight in for his training.

I have, over the years, been obliged to take part in JEWTs – jungle exercises without trees – and even DEWDs (desert exercises without dunes). Others included, memorably, a NEWD – night exercise without darkness – during which, as second lieutenants under training, we were required to transit Woodbury Common's numerous obstacles wearing blindfolds.

The TEWT – tactical exercise without troops – is well-known to military officers while, sadly, our maritime forces seem to be heading for a series of NEWS, or naval exercises without ships. I once conducted a SLEWP, appropriately named for the yacht club in which I was lecturing. When the projector broke during the second of 50 slides I was forced to continue with a slide show extravaganza without pictures.

…

Published

15th January 2010

[Totally erroneous statement made by an MP.]

In his letter concerning force levels available for combat, Kevan Jones MP (Letters January 15) says that *Regardless, all deploy at the required strength for the task they are asked to complete.* What typically-insulting rubbish.

One of the many tasks '*they are asked to complete*' is that of an infantry battalion at war. During Operation *Herrick Five*, 42 Commando, Royal Marines had its force level capped by the government at 555 when its planned fighting strength, and the strength at which it trains, was - and remains - in the region of 608. The same capping applied to the commandos during Operation *Herrick Nine* and I have no doubt the same for the army's battalions during the other *Herricks*.

The fighting strength of a battalion - or commando - is not an arbitrary figure to be adjusted by a government to suit disingenuous politics and especially not prior to a complicated, six-month battle. It is a figure that has been agreed through empirical experience over many years to ensure success on the battlefield via a balanced matrix that starts with - in the Commando Brigade - an eight-man section. When the politicians reduce this to six, the knock-on effect is felt upwards through the whole unit but never more so than when in a fire-fight.

Interviewing Royal Marines back from Helmand I have not yet heard one complaint about their role, their kit or the lack of helicopters. The only adverse comments I receive are towards politicians for not allowing them, quite inexplicably, to fight with the correct number of men to achieve their government-given mission. Less men, paradoxically, usually leads to more casualties.

...

Published

and repeated in *The Week* and on Facebook.

4th November 2017

The new Secretary of State for Defence says that he wants to see the armed forces 'properly represent the modern society that they defend'. I welcome him warmly and wish him luck but with, if I may, an observation.

I can only speak for my own service - yet almost certainly other elite organisations such as the Parachute Regiment and special forces will agree - when I say that the Royal Marines should never reflect, or represent, modern society nor should they ever be regarded as an all-inclusive employer.

In the Royal Marines we refuse entry to members of the communist party, the middle-aged, the deaf, the blind, the mentally ill, the physically deformed, the drug addicted, the short, the fat, the infirm and the uneducated. We recruit officers and men whom we gauge, in advance through rigorous pre-entry tests, to be capable of reaching a state of supreme mental and physical fitness. Then we train them to kill with their bare hands, to handle lethal weapons, to survive in arduous conditions with little but their wits and determination and to live for long periods away from home and all associated comforts. In short we train them to fight, to go to war. This is our business.

I trust that this is not the job description of a normal, all-inclusive employer or a representation of modern society.

...

8th December 2021

[Appointment of Admiral Radakin as Chief of the Defence Staff.]

On November 4 2021 you were kind enough to publish a letter of mine (see above) refuting the then newly appointed Secretary of State for Defence's views that he, Gavin Williamson, wanted to see the 'armed forces properly represent the modern society that they defend'. Now we have the newly appointed Chief of the Defence Staff exhorting the armed forces to do the same by embracing a policy of 'greater diversity' to prevent ridicule.

Since when have the Royal Navy, Royal Marines, army and the Royal Air Force been required to reflect the standards of modern civilian society? The opposite must be the norm with the armed forces setting the highest possible values as a war-fighting and peace-keeping organisation in the, perhaps forlorn hope, that modern society would take note.

I can only paraphrase what I wrote in 2017 when I said that the armed forces can never reflect, or represent, modern society nor can they ever be regarded as an all-inclusive, diverse employer. Winning and/or preventing wars is why the armed forces exist. They should not be diverted from these noble aims by shouldering some rather dubious minority views.

…

21st May 2019

Published

The removal of Commodore Nick Cooke-Priest as Commanding Officer of HMS *Queen Elizabeth* would appear to be serious public relations wound self-inflected by the navy's senior commanders.

As HMS *Prince of Wales* is about to lose her own Commanding Officer may I suggest that, to save face all round, the highly popular Nick Cook-Priest be 're-assigned' to her command where his undoubted experience and unique knowledge of carrier operations will be urgently needed to fill this unexpected gap.

…

24th April 2020

Grant Shapps in charge of our defence! May God help us if that really is the best the Conservative Party can come up with.

…

Published

and then repeated on Facebook.

19th March 2021

In 1982 on Ascension Island a priority call was received for 12 knives. For one overworked supply officer this simple request was one too many. Irritably he demanded to know why a small order for an everyday item deserved his 'immediate' attention. The reply was equally swift and apologetic. The Special Boat Service, sailing south that night, amended their request. *Reference 12 knives. These are 'knives, stabbing' not 'knives, eating'.* The request was met with alacrity.

…

30th March 2008

Published

I doubt that the army commanders are as furious at expenditure on equipment for the other services as you suggest.

The current conflicts may well be "mainly fought by soldiers" but during the planned lifetime of the new carriers different campaigns will be waged with forces less and less able to rely on local airfields and ports. Many outwardly friendly nations feel that offering such facilities in the age of terrorism and asymmetric warfare risks their own security. Carriers and sea-based logistics will become even more necessary as will the escorts to defend them. Meanwhile above Helmand the RAF's ageing *Nimrods* are an indispensable intelligence asset for the conduct of modern ground operations.

All three services are in this together.

…

16th June 2009

[Continuing arguments on the need for the Queen Elizabeth class aircraft carriers.]

DG Rouse (Letters June 14) will need to be more inventive when trying to find reasons to scrap the Royal Navy's new aircraft carriers. It would help, too, if he studied history and pondered the future before offering the quaint notion that, 'the UK with its numerous airfields and flexibility' is the only carrier we need.

Mainland Britain was indeed useful in that role during the European phase of the Second World War but not much use in the Far East nor when the aerial protection of the Malta convoys was vital for our success in North Africa and, eventually, in southern Europe. Neither the air strikes against the Italian Navy at Taranto nor the protection of the Arctic and Atlantic convoys could have been launched from Hampshire: the *Bismarck* was not crippled by *Swordfish* flying out of Brize Norton.

Britain's airbases were of no help during the Korean War nor at Suez when, respectively, fixed-wing and then fixed- and rotary-wing support flew from carriers. During the Malaya Campaign and Confrontation with Indonesia the Fleet Air Arm, operating from fixed-wing and eventually helicopter carriers - the Commando Ships - provided tactical and logistic support for the Royal Marines and the army. Nor were our island's airfields of any direct operational use during the Falklands campaign. The RAF's long range bombing missions took off from Ascension Island while close air support for ground troops, plus air defence of the Task Force, was launched from carriers.

The same argument applies during this protracted, volatile post-cold war period. Clear signs indicate that over the projected life span of the new carriers we shall need to defend our interests far beyond the range of any UK-based aircraft.

As a prime element in today's philosophy of Expeditionary Warfare the Royal Navy will continue to support ground forces in the Middle East and - if the omens, added to a brief glance at the world's many slippery slopes, are correct - in new conflicts even further from the United Kingdom. Here, forces of all three (some would have two!) services will be obliged to depend less on Host Nation Support. Points of entry and logistic distribution centres can no longer be guaranteed as many outwardly friendly nations feel that by offering these facilities they risk terrorist - or even state-sponsored - reprisals.

Lacking this 'local' help, sea-based logistics and sea-based air support will be the norm in the initial - possibly all - stages of any future campaign. Without carriers to enable the military to 'open the door' - capturing ports, beaches and airfields - the ground troops could be denied any pretence of air parity, let alone air superiority. In such an example the opening phase of a conflict will be even more bloody than it undoubtedly will and made worse as ground attack and air defence-aircraft could be forced to transit a lengthy and possibly hostile airspace. When - if - they arrive they will have a limited 'time on target'.

Added to which. recent experience shows that roughly 86 per cent of all *materiel* needed for modern warfare travels by sea at some stage. Without the flexibility of sea-based air cover who will protect this civilian fleet while on passage and unloading in a combat zone?

The MOD should be equipping itself for conflicts way beyond Afghanistan - metaphorically and geographically - with the three services acting in concert and not within individual pockets of self-interest: they, together, should be planning to deploy the complete range of complementary military options available based on tri- not single-service assessments. To cater for all possibilities these options must include aircraft carriers and 'commando-ships' with Royal Navy and Royal Marines fixed- and rotary-wing pilots embarked; aviators who, uniquely, understand both sea and land warfare.

Whether or not the Government will supply the funds to do so remains, tragically and irresponsibly, doubtful and yet it is the future's perceived threats that should be 'driving the defence establishment towards rationalisation' not finance as has been suggested (7 June) by the outgoing Chief of the Air Staff.

Editor *Jane's Amphibious and Special Forces* 1997 to 2013.

...

21st September 2009

[The Royal Navy in the Battle of Britain.]

Your notice of yesterday's Battle of Britain service in Westminster Abbey singularly failed to mention the attendance of the First Sea Lord, Admiral Sir Mark Stanhope, and Brigadier Mark Noble, Commanding Officer of the Royal Naval Air Station, Yeovilton.

The First Sea Lord represented the Royal Navy's invaluable contribution to the Battle of Britain while, more specifically, Brigadier Noble represented the 55 Fleet Air Arm pilots (including three Royal Marines) from 804, 808 Naval Air Squadrons and individual attachments to RAF squadrons, nine of whom were killed.

Lest we forget.

A Fleet Air Arm aviator in the Battle of Britain

...

19th March 2021

For the Queen's Platinum Jubilee in London the army are Trooping the Colour and the RAF conducting a fly past – but where is the Royal Navy's contribution? As the Fleet Air Arm controls roughly one third of the country's operational aircraft and as it shot down in combat the only enemy planes since before the accession surely there has to be a place for the Senior Service: if not for warships on the Thames then for Royal Navy fixed and rotary wings flying over it as part of a tri-service fly past.

…

29th December 2023

[Following the deployment of HMS *Trent* to Guyana.]

When he describes Great Britain as 'decedent, rotten, ex-empire' President Maduro of Venezuela is, tragically, not far from speaking the truth. HMS *Trent* is a noble vessel indeed but at a mere 2,000 tonnes and armed only with light weapons she is unlikely to frighten the Venezuelan horses. Even the 50 Royal Marines that she is fitted to carry do not compare with the Venezuelan Marine Corps which could call on its 11,000 members!

The Venezuelan navy has a modest but potent amphibious capability well-practiced in riverine operations with amphibious fighting vehicles and tanks all backed up by modern patrol vessels, a su*b*marine and a fine collection of missile-armed, fast attack craft.

Precisely when we need to deploy the Royal Navy's Amphibious Readiness Group both of the assault ships, pivotal to such operations, HMSs *Bulwark* and *Albion*, are together in deep maintenance. How on earth, especially in these times (in any times) was this allowed to happen?

Editor *Jane's Amphibious and Special Forces* 1997 to 2013.

…

21st December 2022

[Following a picture taken during the ambulance strike where the 'soldiers' were wrongly described.]

'Military personnel from the Household Division' my foot! They are Royal Marine commandos and part of the naval service.

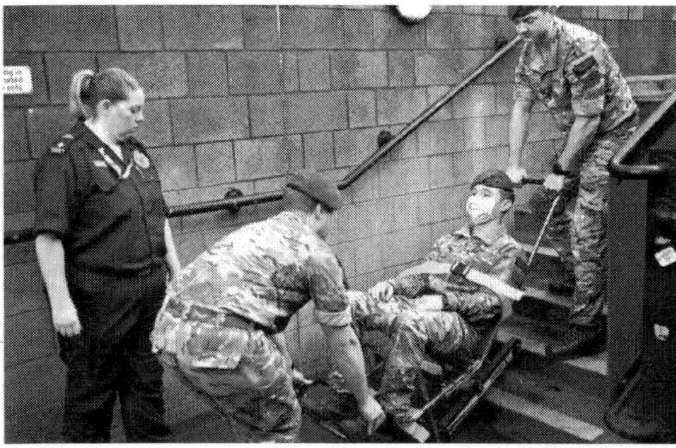

...

Published

(in part) in the *Daily Mail.*

8th January 2024

[Following a report that the Secretary of State for Defence had asked the First Sea Lord to justify the existence of the Royal Marines.]

After precisely 360 years I find it alarming in the extreme that the Secretary of State for Defence has, in effect and naively, asked the First Sea Lord to justify the existence of the Royal Marines, especially at a time of increasing maritime tension.

Just a swift glance at our journal *The Globe & Laurel* would show Mr Shapps just how wide spread, and globally, our small Corps is whether it be in counter-narcotic operations, ship boarding operations, maritime security operations, special forces operations or the hard-worked band service - and that before I mention the invaluable and irreplaceable role of the Commando Brigade itself. Who or what would replace the Royal

Marines for tasks that will still exist and, as we are seeing, will multiply? The Royal Marines are unique and, frankly, carryout out a remarkably varied number of duties that, quite simply, cannot be undertaken by others without lengthy and hugely intensive training.

Leave us to get on with the job!

The Falkland Islands - War and Peace

Between 1978 and 1979 we lived in the Falkland Islands during which time I was able to study many of the beaches and possible landing places for yachtsmen and amphibious operations. On my return to the United Kingdom I sent about 1000 photographs and a 120 page, A4 notebook to the Royal Navy's Chief Hydrographer crammed with sketches and navigational notes. His reply was: *These are the amateur jottings of an itinerant yachtsman and thus are of no interest to this Department."* Three years later…!

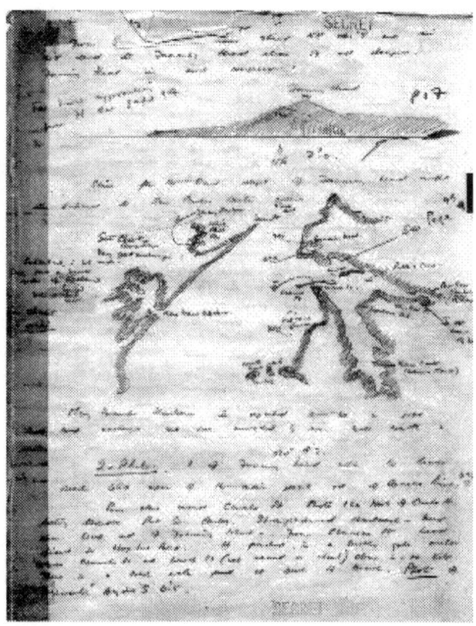

…

As mentioned above I spent a year in the Falkland Islands commanding the resident naval party of 42 Royal Marines with the remit to re-write the Standard Operating Procedures in case of a landing by Argentine forces. I wrote many letters back to the Defence Intelligence Service in the Ministry of Defence (MOD) about the problems we faced with the governor and the likelihood of an invasion. It is of interest that the governor was being briefed by a different section of the Foreign and Commonwealth Office (FCO) than the one that was briefing the MOD and thus me. His openly declared view was that he would meet any invaders with a cup of tea… hence he would not let me carry out my orders from the MOD. Here are some snippets:

…

Acknowledged

Mid October 1978

[To the Fleet Royal Marines Office (FRMO) on the staff of the Commander-in-Chief Fleet following his visit to the Falkland Islands.]

I thought it time to let you know things have been going since your visit as I am worried that we could be losing the momentum… You will be interested to know that His Excellency considered your visit to have been a waste of time. He pays only lip service to our presence and continues to demand that we keep a very low profile for fear that any move we make will panic the public – hence talk of a new barracks… would appear, to his eyes, to indicate an escalation of the threat (from Argentina)… I have fought and fought to be given regular briefings but am simply told that it is his job to decide when I should receive information. What a way to run a deterrent. The politicians and the FCO are the biggest threats to the defence of these islands… Why doesn't he come clean and tell the FCO, the MOD and the islanders that he doesn't want the military here except as cheap labour… Certainly our military position at the moment is verging on the farcical.

…

Acknowledged

End October 1978

To the FRMO

The governor does not want us to be seen to be doing anything military as he thinks it will arouse suspicion among the islanders (and the Argentineans) so we are drastically curtailed although the locals do expect us to meet any contingency. They are always asking what we can do in an emergency and state that we would be useless because of our numbers but when I ask the governor to allow us to practice I am told no for fear of giving rise to speculation… the overt Argentinean presence has begun to give me cause for worry… We are waiting to see if Argentina and Chile go to war on Thursday. It might affect us considerably.

…

[About this time HMS *Endurance* was preparing to sail from the UK for the southern hemisphere so I wrote to her First Lieutenant:]

Is there any chance that you can bring a pig (dead) for which I will pay you and a stilton or two plus a brace of pheasants (also dead) in your deep freeze for the New Year.

…

13th February 2013

Robert Readman perpetuates an unfortunate myth. (Letters February13) I have just completed a three-year study into the 'Exocet war' of 1982 and can state, firmly, that France did not 'provide' Argentina with air-launched *Exocet* missiles once the Falklands campaign had started. Those five that she had delivered prior to 1982 were part of a number of bona fide commercial contracts similar to the United Kingdom, for instance, selling two Type 42 destroyers (one ex-Royal Navy and one built under licence in Argentina) knowing that they would be fitted with surface-launched Exocets.

Within four days of the occupation of the Falkland Islands President Mitterrand placed an embargo on further exports of *matériel* to Argentina. This included the ten remaining air-launched Exocets of the original order of 15. At the same time Mitterrand prevented a team from Aerospatiale flying to Argentina to help marry-up the aircraft with their missiles.

Although a technical party from Dassault were already *in situ* they were allowed to stay until they knew at which airfield (Rio Grande) the Super Étendards would be based: the team was then summoned home to France bearing invaluable information that was immediately passed to the British Government, thence onwards to the Task Force.

Furthermore, the *Direction Générale De La Sécurité Extérieure* aided our own Secret Intelligence Service in conducting a series of successful operations, mostly in France, to prevent any 'black market' missiles reaching Buenos Aires.

Additionally, at the very beginning of hostilities, France sent a Super Étendard across the Channel in order that our Harriers could practice air-to-air combat against the very aircraft that would launch the few Exocets that Argentina did have.

There is no doubt that French-built Exocets caused the Task Force considerable damage but this was due to Argentine ingenuity and not to French perfidy.

…

4th May 2022

I do not know whether or not the Exocets missiles had a kill-switch but what I do know is my book *Exocet Falklands* (Pen and Sword 2014) studied the whole Exocet saga in as close detail as was possible, including input from a number of Argentine Étendard pilots. I believe it remains the only publication dedicated wholly to the Exocet 'war'.

I also give much credit for the support that France gave the United Kingdom – including sending their own fighter aircraft across the channel to practice air interception with ours.

We should also remember that the Royal Navy operated Exocets up until 2002 and thus I cannot help thinking that had there been a kill-switch facility we would have known.

War is a risk-taking business so perhaps as a summary, and *pace* those who were killed or maimed, I should quote Hugh Bicheno (a noted historian on the Falklands conflict) who said, 'The Royal Navy was in a 'blue funk' throughout the campaign over (only) five missiles, an attitude that almost caused a squadron of SAS to be sent to destroy the missile-carrying Super Étendards at their mainland base.'

…

3rd August 2023

Those who continue to believe that France supported Argentina with the supply of Exocet missiles during the Falklands campaign may be interested in comments made in a recently-released Argentine Navy document.

On May 03, 1982, the possibility of obtaining EXOCET AM-39 missiles from the factory was confirmed, via Peru, a country that had previously acquired 4 AM-39 missiles, presenting the possibility of (onward) *delivery* (to Argentina) *as feasible.*

On May 05, 1982, a delegation of officers from the General Directorate of Naval Material headed by Rear Admiral Vignale travelled to Peru, (where) they… directed efforts to (obtain) *the weapons already acquired by Peru or about to be acquired.*

The negotiations with the Aerospatiale company carried out by the Peruvian Naval Attaché in Paris, suffered delays and difficulties, but reached partial completion, with shipment (in the Peruvian merchant ship *Ilo*) *scheduled for May 19, 1982, in Le Havre harbour.*

That day, the French government prevented the delivery alleging technical reasons, and later declared that they would not be delivered "because of the possibility that they could be ceded by Peru to Argentina".

Further convincing proof, from the Argentine Navy itself, that M. Mitterrand honoured his promise to Mrs Thatcher made on the 3rd April.

…

26th April 2021

[In support of Falkland Islands food!]

I am sorry to read in today's letters that Patrick Hickman-Robertson does not consider the Falkland Islands a destination for fine dining. I and my family lived in the Islands in the late 1970s when the food available might have been repetitive - not for nothing was the quite supreme roast hogget known as '365' - but since 'liberation' and my subsequent nine visits I have enjoyed some of the finest and most exploratory food ever. Not only is everything local (rice might be an exception!) but the range and diversity impressive.

The tussock-fed beef is as fine (probably even finer) as anywhere; the lamb continues to impress; the locally caught mullet, trout, squid, Atlantic cod and the white-blooded ice fish are superb; vegetables are, now, locally grown; wild rhubarb and celery are delicious as are the jams (and wine) made from the tea and diddle dee-berries. For the more adventurous you haven't lived till you have enjoyed a fried penguin's egg; chewed on the root of the tussock grass or savoured a form of home-made potted shrimps from the krill. Mussels abound, totally untainted by pollution while the freshly-shot geese and duck are more-than delicious. Need I go on?

...

25th December 2020

[Same again!]

I am much saddened that Lieutenant-Colonel Iain Saker (Letters December 24) had to wait for the RAF and, subsequently, the three-monthly supply ship to 'deliver Christmas' to him when in the Falkland Islands in 1989.

Christmas 1978 was one of the finest my family and I have ever experienced. Breakfast was fried Gentoo penguin eggs; lunch was baked mussels from Yorke Bay followed by freshly smoked Warrah river trout. For the main course we enjoyed a superbly roasted upland goose (having first been marinated in a bucket of vinegar for twenty-four hours). Cheese was homemade cream cheese with wild garlic. We could have had (and did on New Year's Day) fabulous tussock-fed beef, or the unbeatable roast hogget which is more tender and with far more flavour than any northern hemisphere lamb. All this was accompanied by an Argentine Malbec and diddle- dee 'port'. Pudding was tea-berry tart, with lashings of real cream while tea, or 'smoko', after a dip in the sea at Gypsy Cove, was krill paté on buttered toast and wild rhubarb tart. I don't remember what we had for dinner!

Fresh vegetables were a problem apart from the ubiquitous tussock grass bulbs – far nicer than sprouts and rather cheaper than those flown in by the RAF although I am sure the Argentine Air Force, our rather tenuous link with the outside world, would have obliged. Everything was cooked in a peat-fired Aga.

What one can do with a dead Leopard seal is, perhaps, best left to the survival hand-books rather than a Christmas Day menu.

With due respect to the colonel I cannot understand why he had to look beyond the Falkland Islands for 'Christmas'!

...

Published

30th April 2007

[One reply to the *Daily Telegraph* (Letters May 7) from the Royal Engineer responsible for the repair of the runway, stated that I was wrong and that one large crater had to be back-filled - that is right but it was on the edge of the runway and not in the middle. I have a photograph (below) taken by General Menendez himself (briefly the Argentinean 'governor' in 1982) which he sent to me in 2013.My letter also brought a mild rebuke in *The Daily Telegraph* from Group Captain AC Montgomery which, happily, began a friendly exchange of personal letters.]

I must balance some well-honed RAF myths with facts ("Bombing Argentina with all the lights on just wasn't cricket", report, April 30).

Bombed or not the Stanley runway was never long enough to accept fast jets. Until the last night of the war Stanley runway was used continually by enemy Hercules aircraft and often by their Pucara ground attack aircraft.

The Argentine Air Force did not move its mainland-based aircraft further north "so they couldn't take part in the fighting": further north is closer to Ascension Island whence the Vulcan bombers operated.

Throughout the war those of us on the ground and at sea continued to suffer the consequences of fast jets operating out of Rio Gallegos, a mere 304 nautical miles from Falkland Sound. I have been to Rio Gallegos and it has a very long runway indeed and would have taken considerably more than a couple of the inaccurate Vulcan bombing raids to have closed it.

Immediately after the Argentine surrender I and a Falkland islander drove the length and breadth of Stanley runway looking for signs of damage and repair. There were none, except on one edge, otherwise the concrete was in as good condition as when I had been responsible for its security in 1978 and 1979.

My friend and I marvelled, not the first time, at the inventiveness of the Argentine engineers putting a false crater dead centre. Certainly the RAF's bombing operations against Stanley airport were strategically useful but of little tactical value to us actually in the Falklands.

'War is not cricket'. Perhaps the RAF of 1982 had not heard Admiral of the Fleet Lord Fisher's dictum: "The essence of war is violence and moderation in war is imbecility."

Bomb crater on the edge of Stanley runway.
Photograph sent to me by General Menendez

...

10th March 2018

[Captain Andy Legg had led the SAS's abortive reconnaissance on Rio Grande in1982.]

I am sad that Captain Andy Legg feels guilty about his performance during Operation Plum Duff. In my book *Exocet Falklands*, (Pen & Sword 2014) significant sections of which were written with his help, I make it crystal clear that his behaviour was exemplary and that it was emphatically not his fault that the operation 'did not work'. Those who should shoulder the blame were the planners at home who did no planning, but who were prepared to write off an irreplaceable Royal Navy troop-lift helicopter while risking the lives of eight SAS men, an RAF Hercules and its crew, on an unrealistic mission that was heading for inevitable failure before they even left the United Kingdom. Quite simple, the SAS command wanted to 'maintain the myth' which I state at the book's end is, *not a wise premise on which to risk so many other men's lives in addition to those whose proud and apt motto is 'Who Dares Wins'.*

The penultimate paragraph of the book says it all: *History shows that Captain Andy L and his men from B Squadron, 22 SAS Regiment, did everything that was asked of them, willingly, professionally and without hesitation. Despite the appalling circumstances into which they were pitched, coupled with the dreadful weather, the inadequate equipment and food, the lack of any form of intelligence, two useless maps and the unavoidable realisation that they were written off and 'not expected to survive' they acted in the very highest traditions of their regiment'.*

...

Published

June Issue 2018

The Oldie

With respect to my erstwhile colleague Robert Fox's article on the Falklands (May issue) he is talking nonsense. The battle for Goose Green was not a 'decisive hinge' in the British expedition to take back the Falklands. It was a false objective forced upon the commander of 3 Commando Brigade, Brigadier (later Major-General) Julian Thompson in order to give the army and politicians – safe from shot and shell back at home – an early victory; as if the remarkable landings at San Carlos were not a significant enough victory (being the most 'decisive hinge' of all) and in themselves worthy of celebration.

Fox's comparisons with the battle of Jutland is also misjudged. The loss of Jutland might well have led to the loss of that war, but the loss of Goose Green – a battle not in the Brigadier's plan – would, apart from the casualties and the needless expenditure of precious munitions, have been a meaningless hiccup. The brigadier's objective was Stanley not a side show stuck out on a limb 708 'Johnny Rook' miles away. One land battle lost in a campaign does not signify a war is lost, just as ships lost did not prevent the Royal Navy, either in 1916 or 1982, from continuing to take the fight to the enemy.

No war is without risk and that risk includes losses, whether parliamentarians like it or not. Had Goose Green not been recaptured the brigadier would simply have continued doing what he always planned to do and that was to let that enemy garrison wither on the vine with all reinforcements blocked while his marines and paras (who would have initially regrouped in a secure position) advanced eastwards towards the primary objective.

To suggest that Goose Green would have led to the end of Maggie Thatcher and her government is equal nonsense. It should, though, have led to the end of those army buffoons in London who ordered the Royal Navy task force commander in Northwood to execute this pointless attack.

Goose Green

…

Unknown date in 2017

Lieutenant-Commander Brian Dutton's citation for his Falklands campaign DSO matches, and in many respects surpasses, other such deeds that ended with the award of the Victoria Cross. The same can certainly be said of the citation for the award of the Military Medal to Corporal (later Colour-Sergeant) Steve Newland for his actions with 42 Commando on Mount Harriet.

What continues to puzzle is the 'allocation' of two VCs to the army but none to the naval service. It must have been obvious to those in Whitehall (it was to those of us 'down south') that, not only were there more-than-worthy potential naval recipients, but that diplomacy alone should have suggested that a more equal distribution of the award across the services - or none at all - would have been in order.

I must emphasise that nothing overshadows my admiration of the bravery of Lieutenant-Colonel 'H' Jones and Sergeant Ian McKay but there were others equally deserving of such recognition. It is now too late for Brian Dutton, other than 'posthumously', but there is still time for Steve Newland's equally calm courage to be correctly rewarded.

...

6th March 2021

I am intrigued by the photograph (below) of an apparently airborne tanker on page 12 of today's *Daily Telegraph*. If I was the weapons officer of a Royal Navy frigate should I aim at the ship as seen or at the place where it should be. Likewise had I, as an Argentine naval pilot, launched an Exocet would this sea-skimming missile pass harmlessly beneath?

The mirage

...

Unknown date in 2022

[I had heard that the film director John Irvin (whom I knew) was planning to make a film about the Goose Green battle in the Falklands in 1982 and had asked to meet me. This letter was not acknowledged and I believe that the film was cancelled.]

Dear John,

I have no idea what sort of film it is you intend making about Goose Green but before our meeting you might care to know where I am coming from.

One: I tried to persuade Lieutenant-Colonel H Jones (whom I had known since 1963) that I should take his battalion to Goose Green in my landing and raiding craft and attack from La Boca at the top of Brenton Loch but he preferred to 'tab it'[4].

Two: If you haven't already you should speak to Colonel David Benest who was 2 Para's Regimental Signals Officer as he lectures to the Defence Academy on the subject with particular emphasis on H. He also knows something of the next point.

Three: It may not be well known but there are strong rumours that the SAS reconnaissance of Goose Green and Darwin prior to 2 Para's attack, allegedly, never took place and thus the information sent by the recce team was false and made up to look as though they had conducted the reconnaissance. Thus H Jones planned his attack based on fictitious information. Heaven knows how differently H would have conducted his battle had he known the truth of the opposition waiting for him, their positions and strengths - and weaknesses.

...

[4] Parachute Regiment slang for a 'tactical approach to battle' or 'yomp'.

Published

22nd February 2010

Steven Broomfield's suggestion (Letters February 22) of sharing the proceeds of oil with Argentina was precisely what was in mind in 1975. To refresh my memory of events I have dusted off the thesis that I wrote for the Royal Naval Staff College, Greenwich, on my return from commanding the Falkland Islands' Royal Marines' Naval Party 8901 in 1979.

Following a seismic survey in the mid1970s it was estimated that twenty billion barrels of oil could be recoverable: apparently six times the then known North Sea reserves. The tentative plans were for United Kingdom companies to drill the oil then simply pipe it ashore to Comodoro Rivadavia (below): an 'oil town' on the adjacent Argentine coast. There it would be refined and sold to the world's market to everyone's financial advantage, including that of the Falkland Islanders.

On 2 April 1982 Argentina forfeited any such collaboration, yet foresight might have saved the day - and lives - all round.

Comodoro Rivadavia

...

14th June 2012

[An historically-significant inaccuracy was perpetuated in yesterday's article, *I said to them, 'No funny business'.* This is the first of a number of letters I wrote on the same subject but for legal reasons do not copy here.]

I am not surprised that Mike Rose projects the view that only the SAS were involved in the surrender negotiations for, in the words of another SAS commander, 'the myth must be maintained'.

Only one, fleeting, mention is made of the indispensable role played by Royal Marines captain 'Rob' (his name is Rod) Bell, a Spanish speaker. Following his up-bringing in Costa Rica, Bell was able to apply his knowledge of the conventional Argentine military mind-set more effectively than any of Rose's 'counter-terrorist, psychological arguments' to bring about the successful negotiations. It was Bell not Rose that first contacted the English-speaking Captain Hussey of the Argentine Navy and it was Bell who then suggested and established the 24-hour listening watch. Bell flew with Rose to meet Brigadier Menendez, consequently it was Bell who conducted the face to face negotiations with the Argentine commander. In effect, Rose with his satellite telephone, was merely the interlocutor between Menendez, Bell, Moore and London.

Captain Rod Bell - fluent in Spanish and the Argentinian mind-set.

...

Published

9th April 2013

Amid the rightful praise for Baroness Thatcher as a peace time and (briefly) war time leader we must not let the facts become obscured.

Alan Mosey (Letters April 9) states that on hearing of the invasion of the Falkland Islands her 'immediate' action was to summon her 'leaders of the armed forces and told them… that a reaction force would be despatched in three days'. This is not strictly so. At the very beginning she was swayed by a number of ministers, led by the Secretary of State for Defence (John Nott) that 'the Falklands, once taken were unrecoverable' while both her Chief of the General Staff and Chief of the Air Staff were more than hesitant to become involved in what they saw as a 'bloody nose for the Royal Navy'.

It was only the lone voice of her Chief of the Naval Staff, Admiral Sir Henry Leach (below) that persuaded her that the islands were, indeed, recoverable - and the task force ordered to sail.

Now that the Thatcher papers have been revealed at last there is still much to learn about that period of the war as well as her relationships with foreign presidents, in particular Francois Mitterrand, over the largely-untold Exocet 'saga'.

Admiral of the Fleet, Sir Henry Leach

…

24th September 2014

In 1982 the First Sea Lord, Admiral Sir Henry Leach, wrote these words following the invasion of the Falkland Islands: *Since here was a clear, imminent threat to a British overseas territory that could only be reached by sea, what the hell was the point in having a Royal Navy if it was not used for this sort of thing?*

Bearing in mind your fears, expressed in today's second leader, of Isis 'launching attacks on British soil if it had the chance' now is the time for the current Chief of the Air Staff to say the same thing of the RAF: Mr Cameron should then be spurred into acting with the same decisiveness as that so successfully exercised by Mrs Thatcher.

...

30th July 2019

For the Iranian Revolutionary Guards to warn a British warship *not toput your life in danger* (World News, July 30) is a touch naive. Had their naval commanders read of the Falklands campaign they would have learned that *sailing in harm's way* has been very much a key to Briton's naval successes down the ages.

At the end of the first day of the successful amphibious landings at San Carlos in 1982 the noble captain of the badly damaged HMS *Argonaut*, Captain (later Rear-Admiral) Kit Laymen, was moved to signal: *If the history of the Royal Navy is a good guide, ships are there to be used and therefore risked. The Royal Navy has never minded losing a few ships in the knowledge that warfare is a risk-taking business. Hitler, Mussolini and Anaya hated losing ships and withdrew them (and in extreme cases scuttled them). The amphibious assessment was that the job could be done. It was done and the losses acceptable.*

Risk taking in war is the British way, adopting (or in this case being invited by an opponent to adopt) a 'risk averse' attitude is not. Casualties in conflicts must be expected – and accepted – if the aim is to be met.

HMS Argonaut with two unexploded bombs on board and two dead crewmen, San Carlos 21st May 1982

Croatia and Serbia

All letters were to the *Daily Telegraph* unless stated otherwise.

In 1993 to 1994 I was employed by the FCO as a monitor in the Former Republic of Yugoslavia while also being tasked by the Secret Intelligence Service.

Acknowledged

16th March 1994

[By this date it was clear that, contrary to UN Arms Embargo 713, Croatia was, with the help of, *inter alia*, Germany and the United States, rearming in order to invade the 'buffer zone', of the Republic of Serbian Krajina to the east. To prevent my reporting such activities I was ordered to falsify my daily reports as the following letter to the FCO shows.]

I feel this may be the beginning of the end of my involvement. The fact that it is all due to the discovery of tanks and aircraft being imported into Croatia by Germany through the northern ports that has result in my desire, indeed my duty, to monitor the port of Ploĉe to report if this is happening in my area. The French do not want to know and therefore do not want me to monitor any ports or they would have to do something about it whereas the Greeks do want to know and thus insist that I monitor the southern ports. The net result being that I have been ordered to continue monitoring by the Greeks, to whom I am obliged to send my initial report on what I find while also reporting to the French that I have not been anywhere near the ports and thus have seen nothing. This is now an illegal farce.

[I resigned from the Mission.]

…

Published

3rd November 2006

May I reply to Robin Harris for he implies that my information came from 'Captain Dragan' when, in practice, every observation was my own?
I personally saw Italians under training at Dragan's camp and later, when in Croatia, I saw Croat soldiers wearing swastika armbands: not many but enough to cause concern. Swastikas were also painted on crossroads and buildings; never to be removed by the authorities. I was also witness to Germany and America breaking the international arms embargo. Greece and France were, too, unhelpful!
The Serbs in the Krajina had rebelled because they were forcibly incorporated into the new state of Croatia without their consent: the United Nations recognised this by establishing parts of their homeland of 400 years as protected areas.
In August 1995 UN forces in Krajina stood back and watched while *Operation Storm* (of which Robin Harris does not seem to have heard) executed by an illegally re-armed Croatian army, seized the territory by force. Historical fears from World War II - 600,000 dead Serbs at the hands of the Croats at Jasenovac concentration camp, near Zagreb, followed by the clear signs of an emerging Nazi undertow in the early 1990s to which I have referred - encouraged Serbs to flee, those that didn't were killed.
I am no Serb apologist but simply believe that blame for atrocities on both sides should be more correctly apportioned.

...

Published

29th October 2006

I can not comment on the extradition arrangements for Dragan Vasiljkocic (page 4 of yesterday's *Daily Telegraph*) nor on the reasons behind them. Nevertheless in 1993, and while working for the Foreign Office in the Republic of Serbian Krajina, I was obliged to keep an eye on him. On 12 December I called, un-announced, on 'Captain Dragan' in his mountain lair overlooking the Croatian coastal plain and, as a result, he invited me back - alone - on 17 December.

During these visits I discovered five significant facts; he was known to MI6 as Daniel Snedden; he was training regular Italian troops for the day that Italy took back from Croatia that part of Dalmatia lost to the Germans at the end of the Second World War; he was vehemently anti-German (he had a German wife!) while wholly supportive of our own Monarch and, lastly but most significantly, he was determined to prevent what he saw as the inevitable ethnic cleansing of Serbs from the Krajina region of Croatia. All the signs were in place: the illegal breaking of the arms embargo by Germany through the importing of aircraft and tanks; the plan to reintroduce the Nazi kuna as legal currency; the growing proliferation of Nazi symbols and even the wearing of the swastika by some Croat soldiers.

He foresaw - but in the end could not prevent in August 1995 - the wholly illegal *Operation Storm* when the Croat army removed every one of the Krajina Serbs from land they had farmed for over four hundred years. The orders to do so came directly from the Croat government with the tacit but covert connivance and practical support of Germany, America and especially President Clinton.

A number of us who served in Serbia and Croatia and who witnessed horrible events there, perpetrated by all sides, believe that the international community has still not cast its condemnation wide enough by a very long chalk. The holier-than-thou attitude of the Croatian Government - then and now - should be exposed at last. A useful start could be made by indicting - and extraditing - those responsible on both sides of the Atlantic for the ethnic cleansing of up to 200,000 Serbs.

...

Published

18th November 2000

In his characteristically robust letter (Nov 17) Julian Thompson suggests that there are more questions than answers to whether or not there should be a 'Euro-army' and whether or not the United Kingdom should be part of it. Here are some more; small incidents maybe but still pointers to greater areas of international distrust.

Why, when as an FCO-employed European Community monitor in the Republic of Serbian Kryenia, was I shown, in some secrecy by one Captain Dragan (below and whose name cropped up recently in Belgrade) in his mountain camp overlooking Croatia, a section of regular Italian soldiers being trained by him 'against the day Italy decides to take back that part of northern Dalmatia lost to the Germans at the end of the Second World War'? Dragan knew well that his revelations to me would reach the outside world but not via the European monitoring system.

Why, when sent to take over the team monitoring the Croatian coast in the Split area was I ordered by my French superior (a senior diplomat) to relieve a regular Danish naval officer and underwater warfare specialist, who he had sacked for spying against the Croats - aka Germans? (He left, but conveniently 'forgot' to take his notes with him!)

Why, when discovered by another team in the north that the German government was, against the terms of the UN embargo, importing Leopard tanks (and aircraft in containers) into Croatia, was I ordered (by a different French diplomat) to cease monitoring the port of Ploĉe, then in my area?

Why, when I explained that that was precisely why we were employed, was I ordered by a Greek (they held the Presidency at the time) to ignore the Frenchman and to carry out the legal monitoring but to falsify my daily reports to Brussels (and, particularly, to the French) to say that I had not been in the area and thus had seen nothing - but I was in fact to continue to watch Ploĉe and report, privately, only to the Greeks if I did see anything?

Which comes back to the most relevant of the General's unanswered questions: will British soldiers be sent on operations with which we disagree (and whose side might they take if the problem is internecine) and could we also find ourselves supporting a similar, morally disgraceful, illegal operation as that undertaken by the 1995 German- and American-supported Croat army's cleansing of upwards of 20,000 Kryenian Serbs from land they had farmed for four hundred years?

European military unity? - don't even bother telling that to the marines for only a politician (who never has to suffer the physical consequences of his actions) could really believe in it.

ES-T with Captain 'Dragan', Republic of Serbian Krajina. 1993

...

Published

27th April 2022

Nikolai Tolstoy is right to raise the lack of surprise at Germany's tardiness in sending support to Ukraine. He might, though, care to comment on Germany's support of Croatia in the early 1990s when, along with the USA, Chancellor Merkel's government broke UN Arms Embargo 713. This helped to re-arm Croatia to such an extent that that country was, eventually, able to ethnically cleanse 200,000 Krajina Serbs from their 500-year-old homeland: generally regarded as the worst such crime since the holocaust. The interesting fact is Russia was supporting Serbia.

...

2nd April 2016

Your report (*Croatia's anger as Serbian cleared of war crimes. Daily Telegraph* April 1) that Croatia condemns as 'shameful' the acquittal of the Serb Vojislav Seselj on charges of war crimes perpetuates the well-established Croatian 'holier-than thou' attitude towards its neighbours.

Remembering that only last week ex-Serbian President Radovan Karadžić was sentenced to forty years imprisonment is it not more shameful that the then Croatian President, Franjo Tuđman, was never indicted for similar crimes against humanity. After all, one of the aims of Croatia's *Operation Storm* on 4th August 1995 was the ethnic cleansing of over 200,000 Serbs from the Krajina region with an estimated 20,000 of them murdered.

This equally shameful episode in the whole sorry mess of the Balkans in the 1990s was only possible with the tacit agreement and practical support (through the breaking of UN Arms Embargo 713) by Washington and Bonn.

...

Published

6th February 2015

Croatia has been found not guilty of 'genocide' in Krajina (Comment February 4th) but it should remain guilty of 'ethnic cleansing'. There is no other word for the forcible removal of the Serbs of Krajina during Operation Storm in 1995. Perhaps the reluctance to indict Croatia stems from the fact that both Germany and America re-armed Croatia with tanks and aircraft throughout 1994 without which the Serbs could not have been 'removed'.

When we learnt that the German government was, against the terms of the UN Embargo 713, importing Leopard tanks and aircraft in containers into Croatia, I was ordered by a French diplomat to cease monitoring the port of Ploĉe, in my area.

When I argued that that was precisely why we were employed as European Community Mission Monitors, I was ordered by a Greek (Greece held the presidency at the time) to continue monitoring but to falsify (his word) my daily reports to Brussels, to indicate that I had not been in the area and thus had seen nothing: but I was to continue to watch Ploĉe and report, privately, to the Greeks.

The Western Morning News

Published

7th May 2007

After 25 years, the RAF cannot be allowed to have the history of the Falklands War rewritten by someone who was neither at sea, or on the ground (The Falklands: 25 years on, May 7 2007)

The Vulcan bombing raids did not, as claimed by Mr Withers, 'result in the runway not being used for the rest of the war'. It was used by the enemy Hercules and Pukara aircraft almost nightly up until the night before the Argentines surrendered.

The Argentinean Air Force did not, as claimed by Mr Withers, "withdraw their fighter jets for fear of losing them". The bulk of them remained based at Rio Gallegos, just 304 nautical miles from Falkland sound - from where they caused considerable havoc to ground troops, ships and landing craft.

These unarguable facts are detailed in all serious, first-hand accounts of the war and their distortion will cause anguish and anger to those who suffered from the result of nightly enemy re-supplying and Stanley and mainland-based aircraft. The Vulcan bombing attempts were of little or no help to those of us were actually there: to claim otherwise is offensive.

...

Published

12th June 2020

As retired officers, who are West Country residents with long standing maritime links here, we are most perturbed by recent suggestions that the Drake statues in Plymouth and Tavistock may apparently be 'under scrutiny'. Sir Francis Drake is an integral part of local history who is widely regarded as a hero of the nation. A buccaneer with limited early links to slavery he may well have been, but he was also someone who developed into a shining light of endeavour and vision in an age of brutality. At various stages he circumnavigated the Globe, paid off the national debt and drove off the Spanish Armada from this coastline to save Plymouth from inevitable devastation. Later, as Mayor of that city he proved an outstanding philanthropist towards his citizens, as well as pioneering significant developments on the moor and our surrounding countryside which exist to this day.

Surely we must protect our national history for future generations, rather than allowing partisan pressures or ignorance to confuse 16th century morality with prevailing attitudes.

Nick Vaux, Ian Moore, Richard Preston, Ivar Hellberg, Peter Cameron, Ewen Southby-Tailyour.

...

22nd November 2000

[Amphibious warfare.]

Now Mr Blair says that the Euro-force "is not a conflict force". Then why is the Royal Navy's Amphibious Readiness Group (ARG) of up to eight specialist ships, supported by as many again from the surface fleet - plus air squadrons and maritime special forces - and carrying the Royal Marines' 3 Commando Brigade, to be earmarked? This Group is costed at well over £1bn, dedicated to NATO operations at almost no notice, designed for combat at its most intensive and reckoned to be without parallel in efficiency if not in size. In common with almost the whole of the United Kingdom's armed forces it trains regularly with similar units from NATO, Europe and, significantly, the Middle and Far East: a fact that further underlines the view that this Euro-farce will be detrimental to ours, Europe's, NATO's and our further-flung allies', security.

As was seen in 1982 reaction times for the Royal Marines' Commando Brigade have always been measured in hours not months. Of course it can take part in humanitarian operations, has done so with remarkable ease and will do so again, but only a Euro-political mind could understand why this potent force should, formally, be placed at two months (!) notice for non-combat duties under a foreign commander: a position that will jeopardise its instant readiness for more serious tasks which might arise at no notice (as they do) requiring the application of real force.

The ARG could be found standing impotently between two warring factions, neither of whom this country could give two hoots for, acting a role better suited to (as Caspar Weinberger said recently) the Salvation Army, while another, inappropriately-trained organisation will be called upon to rescue a situation involving those for whom we have a national and moral obligation to assist?

Amphibious Readiness Group

...

The Times

24th January 2010

[Following yet another article questioning the need for amphibious forces.]

Will someone be kind enough to remind the Chief of the General Staff that, since 1945, British forces have been involved in Korea, Malaya, Hong Kong, Cyprus, Suez, Kuwait, Aden, Borneo, Brunei, East Africa, South Georgia, the Falklands, Lebanon, Sierra Leone, Kosovo, Iraq, the Congo, Belize, Northern Ireland and Afghanistan. All but one of these campaigns included Royal Marines Commandos who were often landed, with surprise, from the sea as the Army was either too stretched to cope or, often, unable to gain that first vital foothold that only force projection from over the horizon can hope to achieve in significant strength. Note, too, that most of these campaigns were counter-insurgency and not state-on-state and yet the Royal Navy was there with its incomparable special forces and with sea-based, fixed- and rotary-wing aircraft plus naval gunfire. Additionally the Royal Fleet Auxiliary and civilian ships, protected by the fleet, tended to (and will continue to) supply the 95 per cent of all *materiel* that has to travel by sea for some part of its journey. Nor forget the role played by naval forces in numerous humanitarian and disaster relief operations in all hemispheres.

The general should, too, be reminded that for a quarter of all Afghanistan deployments the naval service had more personnel in theatre than the Army.

Since Admiral Stanhope has raised the issue, we should remember that prior to the Falklands Task Force being despatched it was only the Chief of Naval Staff who was all for attempting to rescue the situation. Initially the army and air force members of the Chiefs of Staff Committee did not wish to be involved in what they thought would end with a bloody nose for the Royal Navy; but then we also had a naval officer as Chief of Defence Staff. Now the generals seem to think they can fight with minimal Royal Navy and Royal Air Force support: well, we shall see, and I bet they will be as wrong then as the admirals were right in 1982!

'Boots on the ground' are vital but they are impotent without immediately available offensive support operating from a secure base (especially if there is no friendly 'host-nation' close-by) plus a guaranteed, seaborne, logistic pipe-line. There would be no inter-service fight for money if the Government woke up to its international commitments - or dropped them altogether!

Editor *Jane's Amphibious and Special Forces* 1997 to 2013.

The Guardian

25th November 2023

[Not published but three other letters with similar views were published.]

In his uneducated and deeply offensive article it is quite clear that Simon Jenkins does not understand this section of the UN Charter:

Peoples, based on respect for the principle of equal rights and fair equality of opportunity, have the right to freely choose their sovereignty and international political status with no interference.

Even Argentina's new President accepts this principle, hence his stated desire to woo the islanders with kindness rather than with military threats.

The Oldie

Published

Unknown month

1940, Hitler, endorsed by Grand Admiral Raeder, realised that his naval force available to protect a seaborne invasion was pitifully inadequate. They both knew that any such operation would be doomed to failure by the one service they feared the most: the Royal Navy.

It would have been a massacre – and they knew it.

The British First Sea Lord, Admiral of the Fleet Sir Dudley Pound, might, with some justification, have echoed Admiral of the Fleet John Jervis, 1st Earl of St Vincent, who in 1805 said of the French, 'I do not say they cannot come; I only say they cannot come by sea.'

If Norman Tebbit doesn't know this, he should read Peter Schenk's *Invasion of England 1940: The Planning of Operation Sealion*.

Yours faithfully,

Lieutenant-Colonel Ewen Southby-Tailyour, OBE, Ermington, South Devon

…

Unknown date in 2023

While I cannot claim an entry in 'I once Met…' maybe I can offer an entry in 'I was (more than) once met by…'

I have to cast my unborn brain back to Christmas 1941 and to Stobs Military Camp near Hawick. My father, then Major (later General Sir) Norman Tailyour was stationed there with the 5th Battalion, Royal Marines. My mother, eight months pregnant, was unable to bend to place the turkey in the oven leaving this task to Captain Evelyn Waugh who was staying in the house.

Shortly afterwards, on 1st March 1942 and the first anniversary of my parents marriage, I was christened in the camp's YMCA hut by the RNVR vicar using melted snow as the 'holy water' and my father's yacht's bell as the font.

Before what my mother described in her diary as an 'hilarious rum-punch, lunch party' the family was photographed in the snow by Evelyn Waugh. At the end of the long day (it continued in the officers' mess) he gave my mother his own proof copy (well corrected in pencil) of *Put out More Flags* and myself a first edition of Fisher's *Juvenile Scrap-book* that had been published precisely 99 years earlier. He inscribed this to me - although spelling two of my names incorrectly.

My parents were sad to see Evelyn Waugh leave the battalion although my father might have been amused to read in his (Waugh's) memoirs that he (Norman Tailyour) was 'the only officer who treated me like a gentleman'!

…

Published

Unknown month

Norman Tebbit's mistake

SIR: Flying Officer Tebbit perpetuates a well-honed RAF myth.

Does he honestly believe that the (then) largest and most powerful navy in the world was going to watch from the sidelines as the German invasion fleet (consisting of slow, often experimental landing craft and dumb barges under tow) crossed 22 miles of water at night (when air cover on either side was more than limited)?

Following the Norway campaign in 1940, Hitler, endorsed by Grand Admiral Raeder, realised that his naval force available to protect a seaborne invasion was pitifully inadequate. They both knew that any such operation would be doomed to failure by the one service they feared the most: the Royal Navy.

It would have been a massacre – and they knew it.

The British First Sea Lord, Admiral of the Fleet Sir Dudley Pound, might, with some justification, have echoed Admiral of the Fleet John Jervis, 1st Earl of St Vincent, who in 1805 said of the French, 'I do not say they cannot come; I only say they cannot come by sea.'

If Norman Tebbit doesn't know this, he should read Peter Schenk's *Invasion of England 1940: The Planning of Operation Sealion.*

Yours faithfully,

Lieutenant-Colonel Ewen Southby-Tailyour, OBE, Ermington, South Devon

…

29th November 2023

[Comment on a book review.]

I admire Alan Judd's review of *Conflict: The Evolution of Warfare* but must point out that in 1968 British officers and SNCOs were most definitely on active service. He is, though, in good company for the Royal Marines themselves once used this misleading statement in a recruiting advertisement!

During that year I, and about 60 others, was 'on loan' to the Sultan of Oman's Armed Forces with a good proportion of us engaged in the Dhofar War (which Alan Judd actually mentions later in his review). I agree we may not have described ourselves as 'British Forces' but we were deeply involved - and in force!

Late of the Northern Frontier Regiment (1966 to 1968) and of the Royal Marines(1960 to 1992.

...

5th February 2022

If I was offered penguin burgers in a Greenlandic brassiere (as James Pembroke posits) I would be extremely suspicious of the provenance of the birds on offer. Despite being a flightless bird they would have had to have 'flown' some 10,000 miles - or been frozen.

For the record I have eaten fresh penguin and not as a burger; in the Falkland Islands: fishy but palatable.

Penguins by ES-T

…

Published

7th June 2023

By sheer chance, as I was enjoying a corned beef salad in the sun this lunchtime, I turned the page of *The Oldie* to be met with the headline *Where's the corned beef?*

Corned beef has formed the staple diet of every yacht I have had the pleasure of skippering in high latitudes especially when locally caught, shot or snared meat has been scarce. Indeed it formed the fundamental ingredient of so many meals in my youth while at sea. Yes, we called it 'bully beef' too but more often it was referred to as 'corned dog' or, when in arctic Norway, as 'dog in box'. I won't horrify you with my 'serving suggestions' but they include masses of red wine, garlic and vindaloo - perfect when the cabin temperature is well below freezing.

. . .

The Field

Published

25th January 2018

Despite being the most uncompetitive of your readers I still enjoy a challenge and Tim Hickman has presented me with one.

On my grandfather's death I inherited his father's William Powell, 12 bore shotgun. My father then shot with it, I shoot with it as do my son and my grandson. So, I make that six generations.

I can also beat him on date by quoting Mr Peter Powell himself in a letter to me of the 3rd January 1970. *We note you have been left a gun of our make number 7964. This was made in 1884 for your great-grandfather Sir Philip Southby. It is described in the sales entry of November 24th of that year as a best A and D gun with our No 1 patent action. 28" 12 bore Damascus barrels. Left modified choke and right ¼ choke. Weight 6lbs 11 oz. Price £35. P.S. engraved on gold oval.* He goes on to say, *The patent action is the strongest one made without doubt but we do not make it today because people do not like the unconventional these days.*

It happens that I love the unconventional and thoroughly enjoy the 'No 1 patent duck-tailed action' for its extreme ease of opening and smoothness of operation.

The reason why I was discussing this shot gun with Peter Powell in 1970 was that it needed nitro proofing which, I'm glad to say, it passed with flying colours and thus is still in use after 134 years.

I shall be taking it out tomorrow at Gnaton Hall, the Hon George Lopes's South Devon shoot.

No 1 patent, duck-tailed (flip up) action on my William Powell 12-bore

...

March 2020

I am sorry to read of Carina Evans's experience with her undemocratic doctor (March 2020): she should move to mine.

Two years ago I was in my lady doctor's surgery undergoing what I can only describe as a male-only exploratory examination. Her telephone rang. Having replaced the handset she said, "That was reception who have just received a message from your wife. You have been invited to a shoot so I shall be quick." That was two pieces of good news: I also arrived in time for the first drive.

…

Published

November 2016

Mark Murray-Flutter's interesting article on Secret Weapons of the Second World War mentioned the Welrod pistol: he would like to know that it was still in use in 1982. My book *Exocet Falklands* (Pen & Sword, in hardback, Kindle and now, this month, in paperback should you wish to review it!) contains the following passage describing the equipment taken for the aborted SAS reconnaissance mission against Rio Grande air base where the Argentine *Super Étendards* fighter-bombers and their *Exocet* missiles were based:

The eighth man, Sergeant N, the ex-Royal Marine, packed a Welrod silenced pistol known by him proudly as 'the assassin's weapon'. Although its range was short and every 9mm round had to be loaded via a bolt action from a magazine of five, it was possibly the quietest pistol ever manufactured. Sergeant N was an acknowledged expert in its use and had requested that he bring his own Welrod as a 'weapon of choice'. Captain L was delighted to oblige him.

...

Published

21st March 1968

[Three letters were received in reply, one each from East Africa, New Zealand and Saudi Arabia, all confirming that others had, too, witnessed such 'hypnosis'.]

Recently my company was posted to a remote corner of the Oman, where Major John Edward-Collins, and I witnessed an unusual event. For some days our medical corporal, a Baluchi, had been teasing us by producing large scorpions and snakes from inside his shirt. He assured us that they were still poisonous but would not harm him as they were under a form of hypnosis. We, of course, were sceptical of his ability to hypnotise (or, as he would say, 'talk to') these creatures but he denied suggestions that they had been 'milked'.

Our chance to call his bluff came shortly after Christmas when we found a scorpion (later to be measured at just on five inches) in the open fireplace of the 'officers' mess' (beneath a date palm on the edge of a *wadi*).

As we knew it not been milked or talked to we immediately summoned the medical orderly who then turned down our invitation to pick it up. He would go nowhere near it, but instead called for an Arab private soldier, who, he said, would hypnotise it.

The scorpion, up to then, had been definitely hostile towards us and was kept at bay by a long stick. Because of this, we were amazed when it showed great fear on arrival of the soldier. It tried to back away but was thwarted by the fire.

The soldier sat on his haunches with his head in his hands and stared at the scorpion for two minutes. During this time we assumed he was plucking up the courage to pick it up. This was not the case and, after a total of three minutes, he suddenly stood up, turned to the medical orderly and declared that the scorpion was now safe.

The soldier had, as a child, read a certain part of the Koran to a holy man who had invested him with the powers of hypnosis. However, he would lose his power instantly, and permanently, if he were to kill any animal that he had made safe; although anybody else could do so. Indirectly therefore he did kill his victims as the scorpions were to unable to catch their food. Although Major Edward-Collins and I refused the invitation, it was apparently perfectly safe for us, or anyone else, to handle the scorpion. The amazing thing was the scorpion's complete change of attitude from belligerence to fear once the soldier arrived.

Since then I have spoken to others who spent many years in the Oman, and although they had heard of the ability to hypnotise poisonous animals, none had seen it done.

Perhaps some of your readers have seen this and can comment?

...

Unknown issue

[For the Red Letter Days section.]

I do not hunt and I do not fish, instead I prefer to sail in places were other vessels are rarely encountered!

In doing so I have experienced a great many red letter days at sea but probably more red letter nights for it is often between sunset and dawn that supreme happiness can engulf all other emotions. I have sublime memories of drifting along in the tropics under fair weather sails, beneath a full moon, with a tummy full of curry (and a tot or two) and a laughing crew. I compare those calm nights with others spent in an exhilarating crash to windward in a well-reefed, well-found yacht. Other magnificent memories include swaying across the fore-tops'l yard, unfurling the sail of an outward-bound square-rigger.

But the most crimson of all days - although it was, in practice, midnight - was at anchor among Iceland's north-western fjords in 1997. Earlier my son Hamish and I had tried to land three climbers into Depotfjord on Greenland's east coast from my twelve ton gaff cutter that I had had especially built for high latitude exploring. Sadly, though, that year the *storis* - sea ice - was too thick for us to penetrate and so we returned the climbers to Reykjavik.

As four out of the five fjords of Iceland's north-western peninsula were tantalisingly un-charted we then set off through the Demark Strait. It was tough - below freezing and blowing half a gale - but we stood on to cross the Arctic Circle in order that Neptune could board then, having assuaged his majesty's thirst, we turned for the entrance to Isafjôrđur and the un-surveyed fjords that lead off it.

Three weeks later, on the 20 June - the summer solstice - and with our survey work complete - satisfyingly with a sextant, lead-line, compass and no GPS - we anchored in Leirufjôrđur beneath the Drangajôrkull glacier, where it melts into the ocean. Following supper of roast puffin and freshly-caught cod Hamish rowed ashore to explore the ice. Alone at last with my memories of the previous days, with the 'windy-up' gramophone playing operatic arias, with the liquid in my glass a fine malt, and with the sky a startling crimson as the sun set and rose almost simultaneously, I knew I would never feel more at peace at sea… and wrote so in the ship's log.

That evening remains the most intensely happy memory of all, even now after over 70 years of sailing, for not only was our 3,500 mile voyage entering its final stage but it was also the culmination of our self-imposed surveying work that would, we hoped, find its way onto the charts. Even the unexpected 'impact hydrography' - the offending rock is now well tabulated in its correct position - had had its amusements! Here was contentment that no success in competitive sailing could ever match.

…

Published

18th January 2023

I was interested to read Sir Johnny Scott's letter to his nephew Freddie but while doing so I could not help but think that he must possess copies of Major Kenneth Dawson's classics *From Major to Minor* and *Son of a Gun.* In the latter, published in 1920, Dawson writes 24 letters to his nephew John in exactly the same vein as Sir Johnny advises his own nephew! John also 'replies' with a progress report to his uncle Kenneth and so I assume Freddie will do the same to uncle Johnny. I was brought up with these two invaluable books, as was my son.

On another tack, I am now on my third game book, the first dating from 1966 (I should have started earlier) when stationed in the Oman during the Dhofar War. Alongside the gazelles, partridges and sand grouse we bagged I recorded the deaths of my own Arab soldiers as well as those of the *adoo.*[5] This was not, unlike others, to satisfy any personal account but were simply my initial notes for the subsequent, detailed patrol reports required by my Commanding Officer. They made grim reading then and they still do today.

My game shooting in the Falkland Islands, pre 1982, resulted in just one entry for the Upland Geese are so tame that there was no sport; indeed they could be caught by hand. Having plucked and drawn them the birds would then be immersed in a bucket of vinegar for 24 hours and were all the better for that.

---

[5] Enemy.

The two illustrations from my game book (below) might prove nostalgic for some of your readers who served with the Sultan of Oman's Armed Forces.

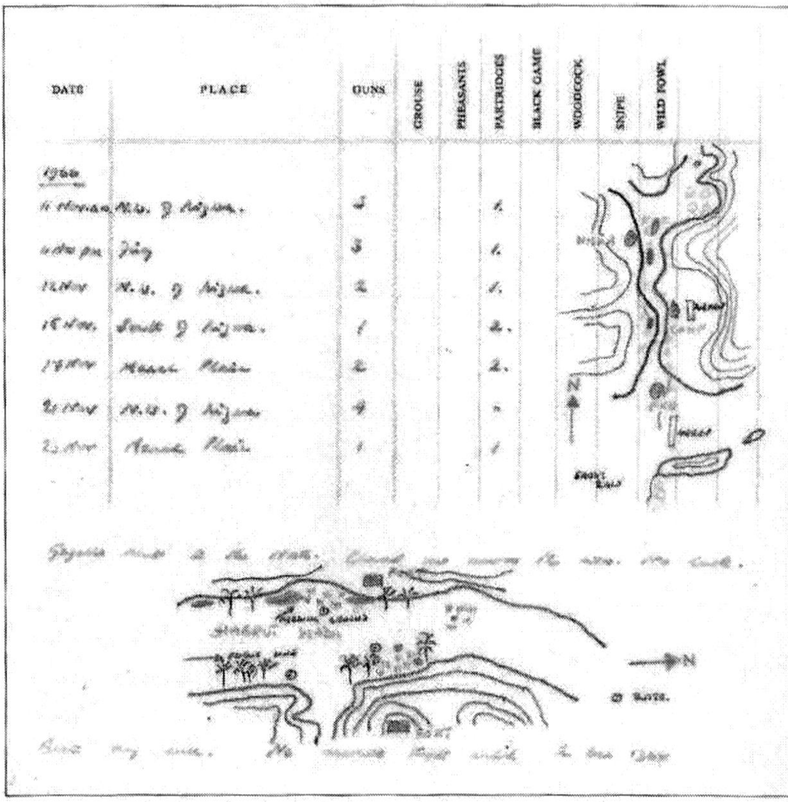

...

13th April 2020

[Referring to a previous letter about the use of Government-issue loo paper in 'compo' rations.]

Jim Gale (letters, May edition) was obviously in the army: in the Royal Marines it was one forward and one aft. Nevertheless, both he and Roger Field (*Defending the Throne*) will recall that each sheet was printed with the warning, should we have wished to sell them in individual lots, GOVERNMENT PROPERTY. They will remember, too, that each sheet had a 'smooth side for the officers and a rough side for the men'.

...

20th October 2017

[The Gun Room at Endsleigh, near Ivybridge, Devon.]

I am not sure if you have a 'roving reporter' but just supposing you do he/she might like to visit the 'new' Gun Room and Country Wear emporium, bang on the A38 at Ivybridge, South Devon. The current website does not show an up-to-date picture - yet.

Last night a few hundred of us from south Devon and Cornwall (landowners, estate managers, gamekeepers, stalkers, pickers uppers, beaters, shooting enthusiasts of all ages) attended an open evening to 'inspect' the new Gun Room which has just moved from a rather small shop (with no parking) in Ivybridge itself to a most magnificent, purpose-built building less than a minute from the A38 and with more than ample parking.

The clothing and accessories on sale are of the finest and from the very best manufactures. They hold a large range of ammunition and weapons as well as offering a professional repair service. The great and the good of the West Country (most of whom patronized the previous, but limited premises) have already 'taken note' of this important - vital - outlet.

Our first and lasting reaction was (and remains) that it is a mini 'House of Bruar' for it serves those coming to the west country in very much the same manner as the HoB does for those heading north. It also has an indoor rifle and pistol range for air guns; there are plans for an outside range.

Although I know the owner well I have no commercial interest but feel that he deserves all the recognition he can get in these early days. He began his 'career' as an under-keeper on the Hon George Lopes' Gnaton estate nearby, since when, through sheer hard work and diligence he has achieved wonders.

I am sure when the cash flow allows he may well advertise widely but in the meantime I was wondering if your 'roving reporter' would care to visit. If not would you consider publishing a letter from me extolling the virtues of this vastly expanded, high class, stylish and very much needed establishment.

...

22nd April 2022

[Following an appalling article in which, *inter alia*, the author recounts using a machine gun to shoot upland geese.]

The other day I sent a draft article about sailing around the Falkland Islands looking at wildlife habitats and a few 'scenes' of the 1982 conflict. This was rejected (I suspect unread) with the rather odd excuse that this month's issue of *The Field* already has an article about the Falkland Islands. In her reply she offered me space for a 400 word letter about my own Falkland experiences. I rather assume that she is joking!

It is almost perverse that *The Field*, of all magazines, should only offer its readership, during the 40th anniversary year of the liberation of the islands from the Argentine military, an article written by someone who does not know the islands; does not know the islanders; admits to being keen to leave the islands as soon as possible in 1982 following the barest of military involvement; who confesses to shooting wildlife with automatic weapons and who even uses a helicopter to outwit his quarry. The last two examples are not what one would expect to read in *The Field* - a magazine I have enjoyed for all of my adult life, partially on the understanding that it encourages good, gentlemanly sportsmanship. I even contributed to your pages as far back as 1968.

My article (which was so roundly rejected) was written in celebration of the islands, their freedom, their wildlife and the sacrifices made on their behalf in 1982. It was also written by someone who has been intimately involved with the islands and island life for 44 years - including ten visits. I lived in the Islands with my family for 13 months (1978-1979) returned with the Task Force as the inshore navigation specialist in 1982 and then continued to visit for, among other reasons, research of the numerous wrecks and to lecture. I also sailed (not for the first time) around the islands in 2003 - the subject of my article. I have also written two books on the islands and contributed to two others.

If Roger Field's article is *The Field's* only acknowledgement of the 1982 campaign, and the islands' unique wildlife, then I think your readers will have been seriously short-changed.

Please forgive the directness of this letter but the Falkland's campaign was the most significant and successful British military endeavour for decades and the islanders and the veterans deserve far better than Roger Field's lightweight piece.

...

28th April 2022

[The same topic.]

I first travelled to the Falkland Islands, with my family, in 1978 for 13 months, returned in 1982 and have visited no less than eight times since to commemorate but mostly to sail, and explore. Thus I find it almost perverse that *The Field*, of all magazines, should only offer its readership, during the 40th anniversary year of the liberation of the Falkland Islands, an article written by a retired cavalry officer who does not know the islands; does not know the islanders; admits to being keen to leave the islands as soon as possible in 1982 following the barest of military involvement; who confesses to shooting wildlife with a machine gun; who used a helicopter to outwit his quarry and who complained that these last two facets were necessary as there was no food other than army rations.

Putting aside the fact that an imaginative cook can, with the bare minimum of extra ingredients and sauces, produce a delicious meal out of 'compo' there was, and still is, plenty of 'food' available without having to indulge in unsportsmanlike behaviour.

For a start there were - and still are - 600,000 sheep, easily bartered with a settlement manager; likewise with the beef cattle. All settlements keep chickens for meat and eggs. Fish, as your correspondent eventually discovered, are plentiful and the ubiquitous, almost-tame, upland goose can be snared using a bolas or, obviously a shot gun - but never with a machine gun. Krill, in season, can be scooped out of the ocean mashed and fried The rock shags, also easily caught, make good eating as do, in extremis, are the penguins and their eggs (the latter, again, when in season although perhaps this may not apply to a hungry soldier!). What a dead seal can be used for is best left for another time. 'Vegetables' are plentiful. Wild rhubarb grows around settlements and tussock roots make a good addition to the table, as does sea cabbage.

In this 40th anniversary year of freedom it might have been more useful and instructive if *The Field* had concentrated on the amazing and hugely diverse wildlife that can be found across the Falkland Islands instead of Roger Field's trite piece and questionable behaviour.

...

Soldier Magazine

Unknown date in May 2023

[Also see Final Essays for further correspondence about *Too Thin for a Shroud.*]

You may be aware of a book just published concerning the 1982 Falklands conflict, *Too thin for a Shroud*, by Crispin Black (published by the vanity publisher Gibson Square Books). I am taking the opportunity to bring it to your attention because I am sure you will agree that it is an attempt to turn well-recorded and academically-researched history of the conflict inside-out.

Let me summarise.

- First, I recognise that Black is sharing lucidly the sad campaign experiences of the Welsh Guards, within which he was then a very young officer. For the battalion, the *Sir Galahad* tragedy - which he records in vivid detail - was the apex of a series of misfortunes. The book has merit as something of a personal catharsis which seeks, and should properly receive, sympathy and respect.

- Second, and quite another element, is his sustained attempt to blame the misfortunes of the Welsh Guards anywhere but upon the battalion itself. One of Black's bizarre excuses for writing his own account appears to be his extraordinary belief that *none of the stories over the past forty years is true.* In pursuing this thesis, very serious and indeed incendiary accusations are made against other formations, commands and - worst - Admiral Sir John Fieldhouse and Major-General Sir Jeremy Moore. These are mainly entirely false and, in a few apposite cases, out of context. Another concern is that the book will simply re-ignite pain for the bereaved families and those still suffering.

Late last year a four-page summary of the book appeared in the *Times* weekend magazine. Now copies of the full book are to hand. A group of veterans close to the events and decisions of the Falklands Conflict that Black attempts to address and misinterpret (Major General Julian Thompson, Rear Admiral Jeremy Larken, Major General Nick Vaux,

Major General Malcolm Hunt, Colonel Ivar Hellberg, Lieutenant-Colonel Southby-Tailyour, Major Shane Cusack, Commander John Prime and Helen Arthy (General Moore's daughter) is so appalled that we have come together to ensure these outrageous falsehoods do not become accepted history. The most effective way to do this, we believe, is to limit the book's 'oxygen' of the publicity and controversy that Black plainly seeks to stimulate.

To begin with we had hoped to have the book withdrawn from publication and wrote both to Gibson Square and to Black himself, explaining our reasons, but to no avail. Of significance, the Welsh Guard's Commanding Officer tells us that he and his senior officers, including Lord Guthrie, the father figure of the regiment, also have tried to stop the book, but with the same negative result.

Although there is very much factually wrong with the book, almost page-by-page, I highlight here merely a few of our major concerns.

The first and most pressing is the opening of old wounds for the bereaved which, after 40 years, we believe is unforgivable.

The second is the clear defamation of Admiral Sir John Fieldhouse (whom Black accuses of lying, on grounds which are preposterously wrong) and Major-General Sir Jeremy Moore (whom he claims, with no evidence at all other than the personal view of a second-lieutenant, was incompetent to command). There is no doubt whatsoever (having spoken to the Moore family) that there would be a host of writs for libel had these two officers still been alive.

The third is that Black quotes from - and mischievously misinterprets - reports written *post facto*, while never bothering (or perhaps positively avoiding trying) to speak to the surviving senior officers at the time, from whom he would have learned through contemporaneous reports why various decisions were made and why they were made at the time. Quoting post-conflict reports is no substitute for learning at first-hand what actually happened and why. As a second-lieutenant Black would not have understood - let alone been privy to - the nuances and complications of amphibious warfare, and clearly he still has no idea.

Thus through 200-odd pages Black strives to blame everyone except the Welsh Guards for their tragic losses on the 8th June. The trigger for the disaster that then befell them is that the guardsmen remained on board *Sir Galahad* despite the strongest advice, indeed direct orders, to disembark urgently due to the evident risk of air attack - this over a period of hours preceding the fatal attack. No attempt to re-write history can alter that basic fact.

Throughout, Black displays an absolute refusal to face any realities which conflict with his own flawed perceptions. Among many is the ludicrous suggestion that, at one stage, two companies of the Welsh Guards were *holding Britain's front line with the enemy.*

Sadly, testified widely by people not Welsh Guards and who saw it all first-hand, the Welsh Guards were ill-prepared for the harshness of the Falkland Islands weather and terrain, and thus did not perform well during the campaign. The original plan was that the battalion should relieve the battle-ready 40 Commando, until then held back to keep the San Carlos bridgehead secure. That the Welsh Guards were instead obliged to move to the forward battle area would appear to have been at Army Department insistence (not yet in the public domain), perhaps anxious that the Guards should demonstrate their fighting as well as their ceremonial capabilities.

Finally, it has to be said that for the past forty years very many Falklands veterans with first-hand experiences of the poor behaviour and lack of battle fitness of the Welsh Guards have been mindful of the grave measure of the tragedy, yet out of concern for the bereaved and the yet-damaged survivors have kept quiet. Now we fear that many will be sufficiently infuriated to unleash a torrent of bad memories into the public domain. This will do no one any good.

With my colleagues, our request is that *Soldier* refrains from giving publicity to Black's book and the controversy we believe it is designed to promote - not to speak of the renewed distress that is bound to occur.

Globe & Laurel

10th June 2011

Readers of the *Globe and Laurel* and members of the Royal Marines Association should be aware that members of the Royal Marines Historical Society have identified (at the latest count) no fewer than nine A4 pages of errors, misconceptions, spelling mistakes and general confusions in Quentin Rees's poorly written book *Cockleshell Heroes – The Final Witness.*

Furthermore, there would appear to be a large number of probable copyright infringements and at least one example of alleged plagiarism. Many photograph captions and titles of at least two maps are incorrect in factual detail.

While these and other unhappy issues have been placed before the publisher readers and members should remain wary of this account of *Operation Frankton.* In the interim, it is hoped - but with not much confidence - that all will be put right in a second edition. Until then potential purchasers are advised to save their £20 and wait for later this year and early next year when two far more learned, erudite, accurate and scholarly accounts are published: the first by the much admired military historian Robert Lyman and the second by our own Paddy Ashdown.

...

18th October 2017

I am both saddened and mystified by Lieutenant-Colonel Alderson's article on page 360 of the September/October issue of *The Globe& Laurel.*

I am saddened, because if all that Headquarters 3 Commando Brigade can come up with in their regular account of what is happening at the very heart of our Corps is a full page lamenting the fact the Royal Marines were not represented at an army conference in support of less than one percent of the population then events have come to a very poor pass indeed. With all due respects to the LGBT community there are far more important issues to be discussed by Headquarters 3 Commando Brigade in our bi-monthly journal: items such as the Brigade's views on current and future training and deployments; the impending role of 42 Commando within the formation; the returning of 539 Squadron to the fold and so on.

The Royal Marines should not waste time, effort and, presumably, precious defence money on conferences and marches aimed at a tiny minority of society, an even smaller percentage of which might, possibly, just consider pitting themselves against our 32 week, recruit training programme. The army's senior RSM seems to ask and answer his question in one go, 'Some soldiers are gay, get over it'. The best way to 'get over it' is not to single out such minorities through disproportionate publicity. If they want to join then they will have been attracted by the same advertising, word of mouth, family members, media articles and press reports as 99 per cent of all other citizens.

So, let the LGBT community apply to join us in the normal course of events like everyone else without such invidious, politically correct, targeting: then we can all 'get over it' with far less embarrassment and, among some sections of society, with far less outright ridicule.

I am mystified, because behind the article, and certainly behind the Commander Field Army's unfortunate decision to lead such a parade, seems to be the view that the army must be perceived by the LGBT community to be an all-inclusive employer. Why on earth should he be so concerned about the perceptions of such a miniscule minority?

And… since when have the armed forces been an inclusive employer? Do we not, in the Royal Marines at least, refuse entry to members of the communist party, the middle-aged, the deaf, the blind, the mentally ill, the physically deformed, the drug addicted, the short, the fat, the stupid the infirm? Do we not recruit in order to train men we gauge, in advance, to be capable of reaching a state of supreme mental and physical fitness, to kill with their bare hands, to handle lethal weapons; in short, to fight, to go to war? If I am right then that does not strike me as being the job description of the normal, all-inclusive employer.

Of course we have had homosexuals in the Corps – some of them remarkable fighting men – and we also enjoyed Hannah Snell's company for 37 years and may well soon welcome the more formal entry of women into our midst – but we must continue to stand by our status as an elite employer and not pander to any single branch of society with parades and conferences no matter how much of a minority, or even a majority, it might be.

...

Published

St George's Day 2019

Terry Sparks raises an interesting point for historians of nationally important events such as Operation Frankton. It is inevitable that, as new evidence comes to light, history will continue to be re-written. Whether, in this case, one believes or not (and I, emphatically, do not) the findings of authors Ashdown and Keene when they discuss, for instance, the alleged rivalry between the Special Operations Executive and Combined Operations or how little Sergeant Sam Wallace gave away (in my view precious little and that for honourably correct and helpful reasons) is another matter entirely.

When Bridget Hasler asked me to write her husband's biography I promised that I would not spend much time on Frankton at the expenses of all else Blondie had achieved in his life. In honouring this undertaking I carried out no primary research from after the limpets had been placed on the ships in Bordeaux other than for those events during the escape with which Hasler was directly involved. I did mention the embryo SOE attack in the book but, purposefully, did not follow this up.

Bill Sparks knew, and fully understood at the time, that his return home did not warrant the same urgency as that of Hasler. Nor did I find any evidence to back up Ashdown's accusation of Sparks' 'whinging': although Hasler sometimes found his cockney sense of humour difficult to comprehend! Fifty years later Bill Sparks made a number of adverse comments to me about Hasler (via a third party) for he did not agree with what was being unearthed.

Inexplicably, and despite valiant efforts by Gill Heard his daughter, Sparks then refused to assist with Hasler's biography and thus lost the opportunity to put his own 'spin' on events while missing the opportunity to add a vital third dimension to the story. Sadly, his own book is not very 'precise' in this regard.

Terry Sparks misquotes me in his letter, the truth being rather more amusing and a perfectly normal reaction for any man to make! Quoting Hasler directly I actually wrote, *The only time that I thought of giving myself up while escaping through France was when I realized that I had to shack up with Sparks.* This was in a 'safe house' with limited accommodation where they were required to share a single bed. All members of Operation Frankton had their foibles, including Hasler himself (whom I knew well, unlike the other authors) but sleeping together was not one of them – for either escapee! It remains a pity that Bill Sparks never gave me his view of this 'price worth paying' for eventual freedom.

In principle I agree with Terry Sparks that Operation Frankton's heroes should be left in peace but I also know that his is an impossible request to meet as long as archives and private papers about iconic events remain to be discovered. How the findings are then interpreted, by historians with vested interests, will always remain a lottery.

...

Published

20th December 2016

[Fictional Royal Marines.]

Derek Oakley asks for further examples of fictional Royal Marines. I presume he also read the letter opposite his (*G&L* November/December 2016) from Lieutenant D. Shoulder-Holster in which case he may remember all the other characters such as Colonel PS College, Major (?) Sword-Frog (?) and so on…

One fictional character he missed will be found in Colonel 'Blondie' Hasler'splay*The Tulip Major* which opened at the Repertory Theatre, Dundee, on 10 June 1957. I can do no better than paraphrase the *Dundee Courier*: *The wartime escapades of Major Tony Corregan of the Marines were… brisk and… even dear old Sergeant Sims found the pace a bit hot… but in peacetime even Burma pales into insignificance. With most of London on their track and a beautiful girl very much in their hair these two carry the day – and the girl – but only just. Sixteen hilarious hours in the life of the Tulip Major.*

The Daily Telegraph and *The Scotsman* also commented most favourably: the original script still exists and I can personally agree with the *Dundee Courier's* final statement that the play *brings lots of laughs.*

I don't suppose your illustrious predecessor as Editor reads trashy fiction so I hope he will excuse me if I point him in the direction of a novel I wrote in 2007 (known in the family as the SSTN or sexy, steamy, trashy novel) called *Skeletons for Sadness.* Although the main character is a retired RN submariner various personnel from a succession of Naval Party 8901 make substantial appearances - however I must emphasize that none are based on those august Royal Marines who served in the Falkland Islands just prior to, and during, the Argentine invasion.

My latest SSTN (in fact not quite so sexy or steamy, but still trashy nevertheless) is called *Death's Sting* and will be on the bookstalls by the time this edition of the *G&L* is published. Again, the main character is a submariner but a supporting role is played by a retired SBS hand. Plans exist for two more such novels: the first, *The Crimson Dragon,* will be based on the work of the Raiding Squadron in Hong Kong's harbour (and 'good-time' parlours) during the 1980s and the second, *Red Ice,* is set in north Norway's frozen fiords (and clammy night clubs) in the 1990s as the Cold War winds down.

I'm doing my tiny bit to keep members of the fictional Corps thriving - even if they are not quite so focussed on their careers as their genuine counterparts.

PS. I know this is blatant advertising but Derek Oakley offered a chance too good to miss.

...

Yachting Monthly

Published

Unknown date

L'HOMMAGE A ERIC TABARLY

BLACK VELVET was the only British yacht to attend the memorial service for Eric Tabarly in the Anse de Poulmic, north west France. She was representing the Royal Western Yacht Club of England of which Eric Tabarly had been an Honorary Member. For her two man crew it was a most moving and poignant occasion and they felt honoured to be there.

Sunday 21 June 1998 was a stunningly beautiful day in Brittany. It was, too, a day of great sadness yet great pride for the French nation when President Chirac accompanied Jacqueline Tabarly, her daughter and other members of the family in a dual service, part religious and part nautical, organised by Olivier de Kersauson.

The ceremonies began at eleven o'clock with a simple but huge open air mass for invited guests conducted by the Bishop to the French Armed Forces on the Ecole Navale de Lanveoc-Poulmic's esplanade. Close inshore sailing vessels, including PEN DUICK II and PEN DUICK VI, paraded in the perfect light airs - no motors were allowed. shortly after midday the VIPs were transferred by Presidential barge through the waiting fleet to embark in the anchored destroyer DE GRASSE. All ensigns were lowered as she sounded her mournful siren and during the following, lengthy silence, wreaths were strewn on to the water to drift, rather touchingly, through five hundred assorted vessels sedately stemming the tide astern of the warship's quarterdeck.

The formalities ended with a six gun salute. Men and women who had, unrehearsed and unplanned, been manning the sides and masts of their vessels, now staged an impromptu sail-past before the family and official mourners. Conveniently, the morning's zephyrs piped up into a stiff breeze. The whole day was, as the local newspaper headlined on Monday, "Le testement d'un marin de legende."

For us the beauty and significance was emphasised by the modesty of the arrangements - an attribute perfectly in tune with the great seaman we were all honouring.

Ewen Southby-Tailyour
and Peter Seldon

...

Published

Unknown date

Tips from the top

Ewen Southby-Tailyour

Has logged 120,000 miles, competed in six Fastnets and entered every Round Britain and Ireland Race

The wearing of a tie is the only real way to keep water from going down the neck – I've never understood why people religiously loosen their top shirt button, wrap loose towels round their necks and are then surprised when they get wet. Incidentally, I wear skiing salopettes beneath my oilskins in the arctic – perfect.

However, the wearing of an Arab *shemagh* is the best way of protecting the head and keeping in the 25 per cent of warmth that escapes from this area. It is made of lightly woven cotton and should be wrapped turban-style and not 'bedouin-style' – by this method there is a 'ring' of thicker material around the head, making an ideal cushion against sharp objects. If it gets wet it acts like a wetsuit or can be easily, and almost instantly, dried in the wind, but down below it is then pulled further over the ears and eyes ensuring a warm and peaceful sleep. It need never be taken off. It can also be used as an instant sling for a damaged arm, as a table cloth, or an emergency piece of light line (it is 7ft long and very strong). I have used mine to help someone in the water hold on alongside and as an instantly available strop once when aloft. I have two, one red and one green, which I wear depending on which watch I am standing. □

...

Published

December Issue 1995

[Proliferation of divers.]

We seem to have a new concern in our midst, the proliferation of divers. Sailing in from the Western approaches late this summer, I plotted a course to take my gaff cutter between Nare Head and Gull Rock, a few cables offshore. As we neared the rock, we noticed three diving support craft flying Flag Alpha to the south of our track. As we did not want to bear away until well through the gap these were not considered an obstruction.

Once committed, and in the narrowest part, we saw that the passage was all but blocked by buoys, but by pinching we could just squeeze towards the main channel of which, although reasonably steep-to was going to be a tight fit. I aimed to give the buoys a berth of at least a cable, so again, no problem. However, at that precise moment the lead craft broke away and raced towards us. Alongside at 6 knots the diving supervisor bluntly shouted (and I repeat his words verbatim): "I order you to head north". He continued to scream instructions at us across four feet of water. Three of the six of us on board were qualified Ocean skippers and the remaining three were all very experienced. We replied (calmly and sensibly, I thought at the time) that his orders were impossible to obey and anyway, we were well clear. I, too, had to consider safety and as we were now too close for comfort (and certainly not for tacking to port) the only alternative was to bear away and towards, but still well clear of, the divers. Our escort remained oblivious to my own concerns and rites of safe passage.

The point is this. While acknowledging the vital adherence to the rules that govern Flag Alpha (I'm an ex-diver myself) there has to be a limit. The divers were, in this instance, blocking a legitimate passage and by ordering me to turn into water too shallow for our draught (and anyway, well away from their marked diving area) they behaved with an intolerable arrogance. As the diving supervisor continued to try to force us further north, we considered either that he was oblivious to the danger that his own craft was offering the divers ahead or, as must be the actual truth, there were no divers in our path anyway, and if they had been, they would have been well outside their own diving marks.

There are now so many divers in the Plymouth area demanding wide berths that yachtsman in these parts have often to sail many miles out of their way on what should be a simple and short passage from, say, Plymouth to the River Yealm.

The freedom of those who go afloat is one thing, but the assumption that, once you are flying Flag Alpha, you automatically have control of the sea lanes has to be something else. I regret to say that this problem is reaching near epidemic proportions and I puzzled over what should or could be done to ensure that we are not totally ruled by these people. We, too, have safety factors to consider, especially (as I when was off Nare Head) in an area where ability to manoeuvre is restricted by wind direction and the narrowness of the passage. There was plenty of room for both of us on that day, but that didn't seem to be enough for the diving superintendent.

The first question, therefore, is what can be done to ensure the divers don't assume that they can just hoist Flag Alpha anywhere they like and expect the rest of us to acquiesce meekly, regardless of inconvenience and danger. And the second question is: who would have had the right away if I had had time to hoist the 'restricted manoeuvrability' day signals?

…

8th June 2012

Published

[This defence of a Jester Challenge skipper followed the Coastguard statement below.]

Peter Evans sailing *Federwolke*, a 22ft Westerly Cirrus, was rescued by RNAS helicopter from Culdrose when his boat was becoming overwhelmed in Force 9 winds. *Federwolke* was abandoned. After the rescue Terry Collins, Watch Manager, at Falmouth Coastguard said: 'The single handed sailor, who had sailed from his home in Jersey to Plymouth before setting off to join the sailing challenge to the Azores, set off his Personal Locator Beacon as his yacht was being overcome by the incredibly rough seas. The conditions on scene were not suitable for a small craft such as this and we do advise anyone setting out on the water take heed of weather forecasts and do not make journeys in conditions unsuitable for their vessel.'

Contrary to the Coastguard's statement, Peter Evans - a skipper in the 2012 Jester Azores Challenge that started from Plymouth on 27th May - sailed in fine weather with a fair forecast then, when bad weather hit him, he did everything right. Despite the Coastguard's report, he had sailed as far as 120 nautical miles west of Ushant after six days of near calm conditions or light head winds but when Force 9 was forecast (and, sensibly, before it hit him) he was already running back for shelter towards the Channel Islands or St Malo.

Size is not necessarily a factor in seaworthiness in gale force winds as many larger, fully-crewed-vessel disasters prove. Much as I respect the Coastguard service it does not help when they make uneducated, nannying comments without checking the truth. Sailing deliberately into a Force 10 is one thing but being caught out well offshore after many days at sea is another and thus should not be hinted at as being irresponsible.

I will defend my Jester skippers and what they do and how they do it to the end unless they seriously do not deserve it, but that has yet to be the case.

...

March Issue1996

Published

[Following an article I wrote about the safety or otherwise of sailing the Dalmatian coast following Croatia's invasion of the Republic of Serbian Krajina, published in the March edition.]

I hesitated to write in defence of my article 'Is it Safe to go Back? On the subject of Croatia as the reaction is exactly what I was expecting, but your correspondents protest too much.

At one point in the article, I say quite categorically: 'there is now no threat along the coast', but the lessons of the immediate past needed to be understood for fear of the future.

I believe, and so do others who have studied the coast and its problems as far as visiting yachtsmen are concerned, that the long-term future is not so assured as the Dayton Agreement would have us hope.

The Croatian ambassador's comment that Croatia has 'established sovereignty on its territory' and that of your Italian correspondent that 'military balance has been restored the area the help of America and Germany, underline precisely why we should continue to worry.

This 'restoration of sovereignty and military balance' was achieved by the near-total ethnic cleansing of 200,000 people who had populated the Krajinas for four centuries.

The prices quoted were taken from AYC's own brochure and were correct at the time of submission to *Yachting World* (as were my comments about Foreign Office advice and insurance premiums). I'm delighted to hear that they have begun to fall from what, even then, very competitive rates.

The small *Yachting World*-drawn map was, I agree, erroneous. In the text I explained that there were areas for where, I suggested, advice should be sought in advance as they might still be restricted: even the United Kingdom has such places. My advice now – as it was in *Is it Safe to Go Back*? Yes, but be prepared.

...

Published

Unknown date in 2009

With 2,000 square feet of canvas set across five sails the 50 foot yawl was closing the coast at eight knots. It was time to hand the spinnaker.

I went forward, wearing heavy sea-boots and with neither life-line nor life-jacket. There I balanced with both feet on the starboard guardrail reaching out far enough to catch the toggle securing the spinnaker's tack. As soon as the weight was released the down-haul tension took the strain, snapping the pole inboard and across my head. It knocked me unconscious – and overboard.

I came-to twenty yards astern and about to go down with heavy feet and negative buoyancy. Then I watched with added horror as Roger climbed over the stern pulpit, shouting: "Don't worry, Ewen. I'm coming in to help."

At the very last second Roger remembered that we were practising for the 1970 **Two Handed** Round Britain Race (and Ireland was added later). Throwing me a much needed life buoy, he quite literally saved my life – and that of the yawl.

Moral: Train your crew to think quickly in a crisis – but not too quickly.

First lesson learned: Train yourself to be more sensible. I did and have never set a spinnaker since: a squares'l being a far more seamanlike, downwind sail!

Second lesson learned: I now wear sea-boots two sizes too big.

...

TV Times

Published

Tales of ships that braved the Horr

Having braved 60ft waves, the gallant tall ships of yesteryear often headed for the Falkland Islands. . . and a graveyard.

AS THE LAST resting place of more than 300 fine ships, the Falkland Islands earned a poor reputation among earlier seafarers, as viewers can see in the *Survival Special* documentary *Ghosts of Cape Horn*, on ITV. But in the heyday of commercial sail around Cape Horn, ships' masters had no aids to navigation, no weather forecasts, plenty of fog and icebergs, almost continual westerly gales and they were relying on charts that were beautiful but not always strictly accurate.

The Falkland Islands' part in this great saga was that they were ideally placed for ships that had been battered fighting the westerly gales around the Horn, and which needed urgent repairs before subsequent attempts. The trouble often was that although the Falkland gales did not have the ferocious intensity of the Cape Horners, they were nearly as frequent and certainly less predictable. Thus, sailing ships would return there badly smashed from the horrors of the Horn to find that their troubles were by no means over.

Most of the wrecks that are still visible around the Falkland Islands were damaged at sea and arrived in Port Stanley either for repairs or condemnation by the local Lloyds agent. If they were written off by the insurers, they were bought by the Falkland Islands Company and used as storeships or were broken up for use as building materials.

The state of preservation of those used as storeships in the Falklands is remarkable. There are
no trees in
islands and t
fore no wood-e
animals or term
This, coupled
the continuous
ing wind, en
that the woo
ships do not r
This reput
for bad weathe
wrecked s
needs to be pu
perspective. B
the Califor
Gold Rush of
very few s
battled east to west around
Horn. Once gold had been fo
the trade increased dramatica
the West Coast of America
opened up. Many of the ship
were lost in the seas aroun
Falklands were, in some
engaged in this trade.
The hulk of the British 42
wooden barque *Jhelum* lies cl
the Port Stanley waterfront.
was bound for Dunkirk from
lao and had a difficult time ro
ing Cape Horn in July 1870.
arrived in Stanley in a sinking
dition and was condemned
scuttled, but not until she
completed many years' usefu
vice as a store.
Another wreck with a fas
ing history is the *Vicar of*
whose hulk now forms the e
the jetty at Goose Green. In
she was bound for Valpa
from Swansea with a cargo of
She was 133 days out from S
sea, when she put back int
Falklands with bad damage.
was eventually condemned
taken to Goose Green. As th
survivor of the Gold Rush da
San Francisco, there is now
that she can still be saved for e
tual exhibition in that c
maritime museum.

Maj Ewen Southby-Tail

. . .

Miscellaneous Signals and Letters

At sea, South Atlantic, 8th May 1982.

Signal sent from HMS *Fearless* to HMS *Intrepid* by semaphore:

The rifle on your funnel badge is facing aft.

Reply from HMS *Intrepid*:

A wise man should keep his arse covered.

The Combined Operations funnel badges for ships of the Amphibious Warfare Squadron should have the rifle facing forward on both sides. *Intrepid's* starboard-side badge had been replaced in the dockyard with the rifle pointing aft – a grave 'sartorial' crime that in earlier days would have ended in copious rounds of port at the perpetrator's expense.

I had pointed this out to HMS *Fearless's* Commanding Officer during a jackstay transfer between the two 'Assault' ships and suggested the above signal.

...

South Atlantic, 7th June 1982

Signal exchange between the leading landing craft of four with the Scots Guards embarked and an unknown warship at about 0300 on 7th June 1982 in the dark following a star shell 'attack' to the east of Lively Island, Falkland Islands:

Unknown warship: *Friend*

Me: *To which bloody side.* Although my signaller, being a more polite chap, deleted the word 'bloody'. There was no reply and the ships turned away.

Four LCUs, with the Second Battalion of the Scots Guards embarked, en route from Lively Island to Bluff Cove in fast-deteriorating weather

...

15th February 1983

[This was for wider, public dissemination in the Islands.]

Monsignor D. Spraggen, OBE

Falkland Islands

How are things now? I trust they are slowly resolving themselves but I suppose as long as the Argentines lay claim to the Islands there will always be uncertainty.

I am really writing about a rather embarrassing statement made by Max Hastings in his book *The Battle for the Falklands.* On page 24 you will see that a remark was attributed to me by Max which has, sadly, been taken completely out of context. I realise how upset people will be and so I am writing to explain how it came to be in his book. I still wish to return to the Islands for, as you know, I am deeply fond of them and the Islanders.

In a 10,000 word article I wrote for the Royal Naval Staff College four years ago I quoted a third party's view of the Islanders. Hastings has chosen to use that one quote and failed to explain that in the rest of the document I recount the fortitude, steadfastness and loyalty of the Islanders.

There is nothing I can do about this misquote in his book nor do I understand how he felt he could quote at all from the article. However as the damage has been done I thought I should explain that it is not how I feel about the Falkland Islanders. I would hardly have asked to join the Task Force under those hypocritical conditions.

I am not writing to anyone else as I don't wish to appear to be over reacting but I know you have the ear of the Islanders and so felt you should know my true feelings and pass them on when and where they are needed.

...

3rd January 2020

[Signal to a long list of retired senior Royal Navy and Royal Marines officers concerned about the future of the Royal Navy.]

Gentlemen,

I wonder if in all the discussions on new ships, advances in technology, future enemies (anyone's guess) and the UK's continuing global (maritime) responsibilities we are in danger of losing sight of an equally important aspect of the modern navy: a navy that used to be famed for the good manners, social attributes and gentlemanly behaviour of its officers and men (*pace* the occasional run ashore that goes wrong!). While it is not up to us - not even, perhaps, for a previous First Sea Lord - to tell the modern navy how it behaves when off duty I still believe that we should concern ourselves. The modern matelot and marine, of all ranks, are excellently trained, highly professional, fully skilled and, rightfully, much admired (internationally) for these qualities but, as our generation well knows, all work and no play…

This was neatly summed up by a late CGRM, Sir Peter Hellings, when he said to me (I was writing the biography of a contemporary of his, 'Blondie' Hasler, who along with his brother officers, managed to drive an *Austin 7* motor car onto Southsea pier's dodgem-car arena!) *…that would quite unnecessarily cause a great deal of fuss if one did it now. The balls aching seriousness of life today comes from America and is terrible. In those days everybody was in plain clothes by lunchtime and the officers and men would have a splendid time playing games or shooting – and we still won wars!* While I would not advocate all of what the General said for this modern day, I can certainly vouch for the source of this 'balls aching seriousness'.

In addition to HMSs *Wizard*, *Anzio*, *Fearless*, *Intrepid*, *Bulwark*, *Rampart* and *Oberon* I have served in (not just visited) three US ships, USS *Raleigh*, *Guadalcanal* and *Mount Whitney* plus a French aircraft/helicopter carrier, FS *Arromanche* and submarine FS *L'Estree*. Thus I was able to judge easily who had the better morale, the better personal standards and therefore, in many respects, by far the better operational standards; and it wasn't difficult to gauge why.

And the reason for my signal… I refer to a letter in today's *Daily Telegraph* by a Mr David Allen that ends *Britain is going to be a sad place if even the sailors do not know how to party.* Quite so but by sheer coincidence I had a pub lunch yesterday with a senior officer from HMS *Albion.* The purpose of the meeting was to discuss the fate of landing craft *Foxtrot Four*, lost with seven (out of nine) of her crew due to enemy action in Choiseul Sound on 8th June 1982. However we also discussed life in a modern wardroom – perhaps not typical across the fleet: indeed I hope not but have my worries. You may all think this is trivial and maybe it is but I fear the tip of an iceberg.

In *Albion's* wardroom there is a cafeteria arrangement (sad but probably inevitable in these days of crew shortages) but, and this is the point, no officer changes for dinner. Red Sea rig is unknown, officers remaining in their daytime, blue working clothes. Wine is very rarely drunk with the meal and "everybody is back in their cabins by 2100 to continue work on their computers". No 'uckers',[6] no poker, no 'quiet conversations at the bar'. The general view on board is that any sign of too much frivolity would be a bad mark. My confidante went on to explain that the table manners of the younger (and not so younger) officers was "absolutely appalling". He expressed the commonly-held view that if you wanted to witness good manners by members of the ship's company who had showered and changed for dinner you had, nowadays, to turn to the senior and junior rates messes. As an aside, I have to say that thrice in the last years I have had the privilege of being invited to HMS *Drake's* wardroom prior to guest nights in the senior rates mess. On each occasion I was equally appalled at the rig worn by officers off duty yet having dinner in such a grand dining room while being served by immaculately dressed staff. I might have been in Joe's Diner on Route 66.

The point I am making is obvious. While even I do not suggest immoderate drinking at sea the ability to relax of an evening with one's brother officers is a vital ingredient of good morale and professional intercourse. Following evening *chow* in USS *Mount Whitney* (where we sat strictly according to rank to eat hamburgers in our fingers and drink the ubiquitous 'bug juice') every officer returned to his 'stateroom' or (for heaven's sake – and it is true) to the huge amphibious operations room to watch (courtesy of the duty non-commissioned ranks) blue movies on the communal television monitors. I witnessed this every evening before being forced to my own 'stateroom' for a glass of whisky and a good book – there was no anteroom in which to meet the officers with whom I was obliged to work. I just pray that (in small steps) we are not about to follow

6 A vicious form of Ludo!

suit (rather obviously not with the blue movies) with the lack of such social interaction and good manners (including a decent standard of dress befitting an officer – especially when in shore establishments) upon which so much else depends.

In other words, harking back to Mr David Allen, where is the life-enhancing fun that was so much part of the vital, all important mix that made for outstanding, professional and well-rounded officers? They are highly proficient, of that I am in no doubt, but something is definitely missing and I fear that we might be seeing the beginnings of a slippery slope.

...

Final Essays

These six final essays, plus a few relevant letters, cover a number of subjects about which I have strong feelings. Thus they deserve their own section although there is some overlap with what has been written above.

As one of seven relatives who served in the Royal Marines it is apt that I start with an essay on Sea Soldiers that I wrote for *Jane's Amphibious and Special Forces* which I edited for 16 years.

Second is the case of Sergeant Al Blackman (aka, Marine A) who was charged with murder for killing a dying Taliban terrorist and sentenced to life in prison. In the opinion of a great many of us this was a perverse decision which, I am glad to say, was reversed but only after a lengthy campaign.

Third is the loss of the sailing vessel *Maria Asumpta* on the North Cornish coast in 1995 after which my great friend Mark Litchfield was charged with, and found guilty of, three cases of manslaughter. He was sentenced (wrongly in the opinion of many experienced seamen who gave evidence at the hearing as well as the Marine Accident Investigation Branch) to 18 months in prison. He then appealed. The failure of the appeal would appear to be a prime example of what can go wrong if the *non-cognoscenti* sit in judgement. I wrote the following paper (below) and sent it to the High Court: unsurprisingly I received no acknowledgement.

The fourth case is the *Sir Galahad* tragedy and the subsequent book *Too Thin for a Shroud* by Crispin Black of the Welsh Guards coupled with the malicious libel spread by Guy Sayle also of the Welsh Guards: both are aired below.

Fifth, an essay written for *Navy International* about the state of the procurement process for naval ships.

Sixth, a momentous event in my life was the establishment of the Jester Challenge and I cover its happy conception as a *finalé*.

Sea Soldiers

Sea peoples, sea soldiers, marines, naval infantry - slightly depending on the era under discussion and local sensitivities - trained to live and fight at sea as well as on land have a history as long as mankind has sought to expand his frontiers. They were used - and are sometimes still used - to guarantee maritime trade, to protect communication routes, to seek space for an expanding population, to acquire land for food, rivers and lakes for potable and irrigation water, to control the source of fossil fuels or, simply in the pursuit of power and prestige.

Down the centuries these duel-trained men have, in various guises and with many titles, been used to conduct amphibious operations, to board and capture vessels, to man ship-borne heavy and light weapons or to establish, secure and defend footholds ashore for future land-based operations. The earliest account of these 'specialists' comes from before 1000 BC when 'sea peoples' fought in ship-to-ship actions in attempts to conquer Egypt while Greek 'marines' from 600 BC are depicted on an Etruscan Vase. In 500 BC Greek ships were recorded as having their ships' companies divided into seamen, marines and rowers while at the Battle of Lädê in 497 (some say 494) BC more than one hundred Greek ships had on board forty armed men specially chosen and embarked for the occasion, thus implying that these were not regular ships' company.

Greek ships of this era carrying *Epibatai* (marines, in modern parlance) also embarked *Eretai* - slaves who manned the oars - and the *Nautai* who carried out all other duties concerned with the handling of the ship. Large bodies of these *Epibatai* could also be embarked in transports; remaining in preparation for a landing anywhere that the fleet might need assistance in its shore-side operations.

The first recorded amphibious operations were the Persian landings at Marathon in 490 BC followed by the exploits of Alexander the Great (who died in 323 BC) which included amphibious operations against Egypt and along many other eastern Mediterranean coasts.

The Romans employed amphibious tactics to help build their Empire first in the Mediterranean and then in England from 55 BC. Roman tiles bearing the initials TR. CL and BR have been found in both Lympne near Hythe in Kent and across the channel. It has been generally accepted that the last of these letters are an abbreviation for the *Tribune of British Troops trained for sea warfare.* The headquarters of the Roman Channel Fleet was at Boulogne where the *Classiarii* - or soldiers trained for service at sea - performed the same functions as the Greek *Epibatai.* They wore a sea-green uniform that matched the colour of their shields: a designed colour scheme that might be considered the earliest military camouflage. The Romans also maintained a small force of *Lembarii* who served on board small war-vessels known as *lembus*: a word that translates into a small sailing vessel with a sharp prow.

As part of their 'order of battle' the Greeks and the Romans trained and equipped men for both service at sea and ashore. In the case of the Romans in south east England, northern France and along the Mediterranean coast these men would have been, as was the custom, recruited or pressed from among the local population. There was certainly at least one 'marine cohort' of between 500 and 1,000 men in Britain between 96 and 117 AD.

Prior to returning to defend their Imperial city against the 'hordes of Gothic warriors that threatened' the Romans placed one of their Corps of Marines under the Count of the Saxon Shore's direct command to face would-be invaders from the north and east: Vikings described by a Roman poet at the time as *Foes, fierce beyond other foes and as cunning as they are fierce: the sea is their school of war and the storm their friend; they are sea-wolves that live on the pillage of the world.*

Once the occupying force finally departed, Britain was left with neither marines nor a navy to employ or transport them. It can be argued that the Corps of Butescarles that served in Alfred the Great's navy were the natural successors to the *Classiarii* but with this brief exception alone the sea-soldier - at least in northern waters - would be extinct, or nearly so, for some centuries.

The 'amphibious' fleets of the Greek and Roman eras were a much closer match to those that exist today when compared to those of the - British - middle ages. Throughout this last era merchant ships would be pressed into service to augment the very few 'kings' ships - effectively also in trade - when they would be retro-fitted (in modern terminology) with fore and aft castles from which they could be fought: some would also carry men-at arms for specific operations. Edward III made provision for a marine force and when, in 1417, Sir Thomas Carew fitted a squadron of 11 ships for service the largest embarked a force of 75 men-at-arms plus 148 archers.

The Elizabethan era was not without its sea soldiers either. Drake's expeditions all included soldiers trained for service at sea and ashore while, with many such deployments, it was not always clear who was in command. Previously, ships were merely used to transport troops to wherever their commander needed to go but with the advent of more efficient sailing vessels it was it was often unclear who was - or should be - in command.

The specialist role of the 'sea soldier' was given a more modern impetus when Spain formed her *Infantería de Marina* in 1537. Portugal followed with her *Corpo de Fuzileiros* in 1585, Great Britain (*Per Mare Per Terram* - By Sea By Land) with her Marines in 1664 (Royal in 1802) and the Dutch *Korps Mariniers* (*Qua Patet Orbis* - As Far As The World Extends) the next year. 1775 saw the formation of the United States Marine Corps (*Semper Fidelis* - Always Faithful) and then Brazil joined the 'club' in 1808 with the *Corpo de Fuzileiros Navais* - (*Adsumus* - Here We Are).

Now many maritime nations possess a marine force of some sort although with very few exceptions - notably the Americans, United Kingdom and France - most do not serve permanently at sea. With modern, fully automated, heavy weapons currently operated by a 'weapons electrical' specialist rather than a 'gunner', marines around the globe have lost this traditional role. Nor do many marine corps have any amphibious assault capability but merely replace sailors for security duties and the defence of naval areas: the word 'marine' can imply anything from the most highly trained amphibious 'shock troops' to local guards.

Conversely, there remain nations with an amphibious capability and aspiration yet no specialist amphibious troops: Australia being a good example although the Special Air Service Regiment does have an amphibious troop within each squadron. There are two reasons why this is so often the case: one self-evident and one misguided and erroneous.

The first is that good marine training is lengthy and costly and the second is that regular army units - envious of the money and time spent on a marine corps' training - argue that there is a bogus mystique attached to such elite soldiers. The *non-cognoscenti* - or, simply, the unwilling to learn - often argue that this mystique purposefully generates an air of false complications in order to ensure that the naval infantry remain in business as specialists. An example will be found during a successful amphibious landing conducted by a tiny British army force from HMS *Fearless* off the southern Oman coast in October 1966. On completion the army Brigade commander voiced the opinion that he could see nothing complicated with amphibious warfare and suggested that the army could take over the role. What he and others in similar situations failed to appreciate was that the Oman operation - *Operation Fate* - was an un-opposed, single ship, single unit (embarked only the day prior to the landings) landing in daylight.

A more representative amphibious operation might involve a brigade, supporting arms from all three services, naval and marine surface, sub-surface, air and electronic warfare, special forces advance force operations, naval gunfire support, intelligence acquisition and complicated diplomatic involvement up until the last moment: plus the rest. The British Army's 5 Brigade in the Falkland conflict believed, as had the land commander of *Operation Fate*, that it was a simple business of landing by ferry and then advancing along a coast made even more simple by re-supply across an open - the sea - flank. How very wrong they were proved to be: a fact summed up by a British admiral at the time thus: *Amphibious operations are at the scholarship level of military operations.* By this he meant everyone involved from all three services had to be trained to the highest level but, specifically, he was implying that the 'sea soldiers' needed to be at that scholarship level: specially trained and able to wholly integrate - and remain permanently integrated - into the force.

It is worth repeating Winston Churchill in 1942 before the Tobruk landings in North Africa: *An amphibious operation has to fit together like a jewelled bracelet.* That dictum still applies and continues to reinforce the argument that such operations cannot be undertaken by an ad hoc collection of troops, ships and aircraft brought together at the last moment to fulfil a sudden need.

For amphibious troops - marines - and their embedded specialists, amphibious training will involve long periods on board ships and in - to basic infantry soldiers - an alien environment while non-amphibious commanders will be equally frustrated by the nuances of naval warfare and the restrictions imposed on their actions up to and after the initial landings. Naval infantry understand this and, working alongside their naval colleagues, are able to fit in, tolerate and even take part in naval warfare operations under the water, on its surface and above it. They are part of the whole: it's a state of mind as much as anything.

While some marine forces are trained merely to protect naval installations, others operate small craft in coastal or riverine operations, land from ships by sea or air for a specific task such as capturing a beach or port – an entry point – to enable later landings by heavy forces. Nevertheless a few elite marine corps have gone further and embraced harsh training to 'special force' standards. The British Royal Marines joined a few army units of volunteers in the commando role during the Second World War: as traditional a role for marines as any as a mere glimpse of their actions over the preceding centuries will show.

Raiding from the sea, often across seemingly impassable coastlines or up vertical cliffs – anywhere but the place from which an enemy might expect an attack – has been the business of marines down the centuries together with manning both heavy guns and light weapons. It was not surprising, therefore, that at the Second World War's end the British army reverted to a standard infantry role while the Royal Marines continued as commandos: a most natural extension - and expansion - of their role as sea soldiers.

A few other marine forces followed the example and if not always called 'commandos' or something with a similar meaning, they at least carried out the same tasks. French, Indian and Indonesian marines all have the additional 'commando' skills that allow them not only to fight by land and sea but to conduct very complicated, arduous operations under the toughest conditions the globe has to offer – and not necessarily confined to the littoral battle space. Additionally, many marine corps go one step further and find their country's maritime special forces from within their ranks.

An added bonus in a very few marine corps – the Dutch and the British are prime examples – is that the navy's raiding and landing craft (including hovercraft in the case of the British) are also manned by commando-trained marines. As with naval pilots in support of naval operations and army pilots supporting land operations the coxswains and crews of assault craft understand the amphibious battle. Far better that such operations are supported by amphibious boats crews as is the case with specialist naval and army aircrew overhead.

...

Sergeant Al Blackman (Marine A)

All letters were to the *Daily Telegraph* unless stated otherwise.

11th November 2013

May I offer two alternative views on the case of Marine A: both culled from bitter, personal experience over 32 years as a Royal Marine in Aden, Northern Ireland, the Yemen, the Oman and the Falkland Islands.

From the beginning of warfare fatally wounded combatants - both friend and foe - for whom there is no hope have been 'put out of their misery' on the battlefield. This has been the case (and will continue to be the case whether the lawyers like it or not) when the dying have no resource to effective first aide to ease their pain and lesson the emotional agony of the inevitable. An overdose of morphine is one humane way and a bullet is the other. Without either they will linger: alone, in immense physical distress and terrified.

Supposing Marine A's finals words had been 'Sorry, mate. There is nothing more we can do for you. May you rest in peace…?' Would he still have been charged with murder? Or perhaps manslaughter? Would his seniors, when confronted with the recorded facts, have accepted that nothing else could have been done and that he had behaved honourably under exceptionally disturbing and desperate circumstances?

I suggest that the crime committed by Marine A is to be found in his unfortunately-recorded words (remembering, too, that battle has a patois all of its own that those who have never experience it will find uncomfortable) and not specifically in the deed.

Secondly, it has been stated that any clemency shown by a British court-martial would be playing into the enemy's hands and make the fate of a captured western soldier worse. This is an asinine assumption. The destiny of a British combatant captured by a terrorist is not going to be altered one jot by the length of any sentence - long or, preferably, short - that may be handed down to Marine A. His fate will remain the same as it always has been in that part of the world: torture, beheading and, finally, dismemberment for public display: it can't get worse than it already is.

…

No response

14th December 2013

The Chief of the Defence Staff

I never thought that I would have to write to a British CDS in these terms and so this saddens me greatly.

During your recent appearance on the Andrew Marr show you said that 'murder is murder'. I must therefore ask you how you would describe the behaviour of the SAS men who killed three unarmed 'terrorists' in Gibraltar on 6th March 1988? I would also ask you what your opinion is on the incident in 1982 when an Argentine soldier was shot at Goose Green as he was dying, in agony, sometime after the 'heat of battle' had subsided. I believe that the Padre was present.

How do you regard my action when, during a battle in the Dhofar War, I over-dosed my fatally-wounded Arab Sergeant Major with morphine as there was no hope for him and certainly no first aid? Sadly, mortally injured combatants of both sides have been, quite rightly, 'put out of their misery' ever since warfare began – whether or not the lawyers like it.

You also suggested that there should be no request for clemency for Marine A by those in authority when, surely, that episode of his trial was still *sub judice*. Your comments – as CDS – would undoubtedly have influenced the court's deliberations on the length of sentence and I find that regrettable.

…

Published

14th September 2015

The Daily Mail

The primary duty of the infantryman is to close with and kill the enemy.

(Field Marshal Montgomery?)

I write in total support for any 'campaign' with which the *Daily Mail* may be involved to have Sergeant Blackman's conviction for murder quashed and his sentence annulled. I do so from a position of some understanding of battle culled from personal experience in Aden, Northern Ireland, the Yemen, the Oman (Dhofar War) and the Falkland Islands during Operation Corporate.

From the beginning of warfare fatally wounded combatants - both friend and foe - and for whom there is no hope, have been 'put out of their misery' on the battlefield. This has always been the case (and will continue to be the case whether the lawyers like it or not) when the dying soldier has no resource to relevant first aid to ease their pain and lessen the emotional agony of the inevitable.

An overdose of morphine is one humane way and a bullet is another humane way. Without one or the other the dying soldier will linger: alone, in immense physical distress and terrified. I know of one case in the Falklands Campaign (I am sure there were others) when a mortally wounded Argentine was shot at Goose Green. There was no hope for him and he was put out of his misery, humanely and swiftly. (I believe the Padre was present and approved.)

For my part I purposefully over-dosed my dying Company Sergeant Major (an Arab) with morphine during a battle in the Dhofar region of the Oman when I was on a two year secondment to the Northern Frontier Regiment of the Sultan's Armed Forces (SAF) between 1966 and 1968.

The CSM had been shot through the neck, was dying in colossal agony with no hope and certainly no first aid. We were also in the middle of the largest, most intense fire-fight then experienced by the SAF. I had no choice if we wished to come to grips with the enemy rather than remain kneeling beside a dying man while the *adoo*[7] regrouped: they attacked us twice more that afternoon before we finally beat them off.

I suggest that the only 'non-crime' Sergeant Blackman committed will be found in his unfortunately-recorded choice of words… and yet what the judges and the public will never understand is that the horror of battle has a patois all of its own that those who have not experienced will find uncomfortable when quoted in the calm of a court room or on the pages of a 'family' newspaper. Someone described Sergeant Blackman's words as

[7] Enemy.

'chilling' but I would say that they were nothing out of the ordinary for men in battle - of any rank.

I believe the judge in Sergeant Blackman's case stated that he was not acting 'in the heat of battle', and thus could not use that as a defence. I would argue that the adrenaline flows (even more so under the circumstances in which we now know he found himself) from the moment you leave the comparative safety of your base to long after you have returned… and what about the *Apache* pilot who was well shielded from any 'heat of battle' and yet who, quite legally, targeted 'civilians'. (Drone pilots may well be cited too, I would have thought.)

Another case is the occasion on 6th March 1988 when the SAS killed three unarmed members of the IRA on the streets of Gibraltar. Was that not a cold-blooded killing of men in civilian clothes who at that moment were offering no threat to the SAS?… and yet no one was charged. I was all for killing them - a fourteen-year-old IRA girl murdered my brother-in-law in Anderson's Town in 1971 - but you will get my point.

Before Sergeant Blackman was wrongly sentenced (by a court of entirely the incorrect/inappropriate composition for such a serious charge) it was stated that any clemency shown by the court-martial would be playing into the enemy's hands and make the fate of a captured western soldier worse. That was an asinine assumption.

The destiny of any British combatant captured by a terrorist was not going to be altered one jot by the length of any sentence handed down to Sergeant Blackman: or even by a verdict of not guilty. A British soldier's fate remained the same as it always had been in that part of the world: torture, beheading and, finally, dismemberment for public display. It could not have become worse than it already was. The same would have occurred to us in the Dhofar War had we had the misfortune to be captured.

So, what was Sergeant Blackman's alternative? Leave the terrorist to die as they, the Royal Marines, had no suitable medical resources with which merely to prolong his inevitable death? It could be successfully argued that this would have been just as 'criminal' an act (it would certainly have been an inhumane act) as putting the terrorist instantly out of his misery with a single 9 mm round direct to the heart. Have we not all seen the videos of

Taliban being attacked by US *Apaches* who then came back to finish off the wounded? What on earth is the difference?

Sergeant Blackman could have called in a *Chinook* with a Medical Emergency Response Team (MERT) embarked so risking a valuable aircraft and even more valued medics on an enemy already close to death. What an unacceptable risk of a *Chinook*/MERT that would have been and I speak as the uncle of a niece who flew as a medic in them.

I do not believe for one moment that what Sergeant Blackman did was illegal under the circumstances: it was, frankly, sheer common sense and I would have done (indeed I have done) the same. I also believe that in the right legal hands it would be argued, successfully, to have been a morally defensible act of mercy.

…

16th September 2015

[Mr Terrill wrote in support of the murder charge.]

No, Mr Terrill, Sergeant Alexander Blackman was not 'a murderer who deserves to be free', he was a Royal Marine who should never have been charged with that particular crime. Was it not Field Marshal Montgomery who said that an infantryman's primary duty is to close with and kill the enemy?

So, what was Sergeant Blackman's alternative? Leave the terrorist to die as they, the Royal Marines, had no suitable medical resources with which merely to prolong his inevitable death? It could be successfully argued that this would have been just as 'criminal' an act (it would certainly have been an inhumane act for which he could well have faced a charge) as putting the near-dead terrorist out of his misery with a single 9 mm round direct to the heart. Have we not all seen the videos of the Taliban being attacked by US *Apaches* who then came back to finish off the wounded? What on earth is the difference?

Then, what about the *Apache* pilot who was well shielded from any 'heat of battle' and yet who, quite legally, targeted 'civilians'. (Drone pilots may well be cited too, I would have thought.)

I suggest that the only 'crime' Sergeant Blackman committed will be found in his unfortunately-recorded choice of words… and yet what the judges and the public will never understand is that the horror of battle has a patois all of its own that those who have not experienced will find uncomfortable when quoted in the calm of a court room or on the pages of a 'family' newspaper. Someone described Sergeant Blackman's words as 'chilling' but I would say that they were nothing out of the ordinary for men in battle - of any rank.

If Mr Terrill considers Sergeant Blackman a murderer how does he rate the SAS troops who gunned down, in cold blood, three unarmed IRA men in Gibraltar on 6 March 1988? Men who, at the time, were posing no threat to the SAS. Or how does he rate the Argentine soldier mortally wounded at Goose Green in 1982 who was put out of his misery with a single pistol shot.

I purposefully over-dosed my dying Company Sergeant Major (an Arab) with morphine during a battle in the Dhofar region of the Oman when I was on a two year secondment to the Northern Frontier Regiment of the Sultan's Armed Forces (SAF) between 1966 and 1968.

The CSM had been shot through the neck, was dying in colossal agony with no hope and certainly no first aid. We were also in the middle of the largest, most intense fire-fight then experienced by the SAF. I had no choice if we wished to come to grips with the enemy rather than remain kneeling beside a dying man while the *adoo* regrouped: they attacked us twice more that afternoon before we finally beat them off.

I do not believe for one moment that what Sergeant Blackman did was illegal or immoral under the circumstances: it was, frankly, sheer common sense and I would have done (indeed I have done) the same.

I also believe that in competent legal hands it should have been argued that Blackman committed a morally defensible act of mercy: a 'crime' that should have been, more correctly, covered by the charge of manslaughter. It beggars all believe that his defence team did not pounce on that fact.

…

9th November 2015

I notice that the Chief of Defence Staff continues to argue that Sergeant Blackman or Marine A (*Daily Telegraph* November 9) has been fairly dealt with. Putting aside for the moment the pros and cons of this case the one question that no one has yet answered is what should Blackman have done instead.

Let me, as someone who has been in the sergeant's position (Dhofar War, 1968) suggest the very limited choices that were available to him.

First. He could have prevented the terrorist from dying through the application of first aid but why prolong the inevitable at further risk to one self. Additionally, the patrol had nothing with which to do this. The only morphine ampoules available were individual ones not to be used on anyone else. His back wound (courtesy of an *Apache*) was, simply, untreatable.

Second. He could have called in a *Chinook* with an on-board Medical Emergency Response Team (MERT). By the time it would have arrived the terrorist, if not dead already, would certainly have died. This would have been an unacceptable risk of an invaluable asset with no likelihood of a positive outcome.

Third. Blackman and his team could have dragged the terrorist to safety. While this might have been safe for the terrorist in his dying moments, while the team held his hand, it would still keep Sergeant Blackman's patrol in the general killing zone; an area best left as soon as possible. If that means leaving a dying enemy behind then so be it. The safety of one's own men is paramount, not that of a dying terrorist. It was imperative to get away from the area as soon as possible to regroup elsewhere in order to engage the enemy on your own terms.

Fourth. Blackman could put the terrorist out of his misery so that the patrol might leave the killing zone and get on with its task. This has been the common sense choice used down the centuries for friend and foe alike. But how? Three more choices were available to the patrol commander. One. Get on with the patrol and let the terrorist die in his own time: an inhumane act that would have brought deserved opprobrium. Two. Administer an overdose of morphine: peaceful but a danger of being charged with murder. Three. Fire a single 9 mm bullet direct to the heart: instant but a danger of being charged with murder.

Will someone now tell me which choice they would have taken and why…or are there any others I have failed to spot?

It strikes me that Sergeant Blackman has been condemned by words which are quite normal as part of the 'patois of battle'. Things are said before, during and after a fire fight - for bravado, for effect, for release of tension - that should never be produced in the calm of a court to be used for damnation by the *non-cognoscenti*. The heat of battle does not evaporate the moment the last round has been fired for it is then that the adrenaline, the fear, the nervousness often become far more intense.

…

22nd September 2016

Following on from Mr Frederick Forsyth's letter (Letters September 22) there is another aspect to Sergeant Blackman's case that has never been addressed. What should he have done? The following essay may help to answer this vital question:

Sergeant Alexander Blackman Royal Marines
OPTIONS
and
OBSERVATIONS

Putting aside, for a moment, Sergeant Blackman's defence team failing to ask for the alternative charge of manslaughter to be brought, the rumour that members of the court martial's panel were told to find him guilty, coupled to the alleged suppression of evidence for his defence, there is another factor in this unique and disturbing case. Quite simply, what else was Sergeant Blackman supposed to do with a mortally wounded terrorist?

Very few have condemned Sergeant Al Blackman while many, many thousands are supporting his bid for a review yet no one (on either 'side') has been prepared to say what he should have done. A number have commented adversely on his actions but unless they can answer this question their statements are shallow to the point of being meaningless.

So, let me as, then, the Second in Command of 3 Company, the Desert Regiment, the Sultan of Muscat's Armed Forces (on loan from A Company, the Northern Frontier Regiment - which I was commanding) offer a few suggestions based on my own experience. On the 11th January 1968 during the Dhofar War and in the middle of a fire fight (the first of three that day, of many days) I put to sleep my mortally wounded Arab (Muslim) Sergeant Major with an overdose of morphine. On reflection I had roughly the same choices available to me in 1968 as, I would suggest, Sergeant Blackman had on the 15th December 2011 in Helmand. His were these:

First. Prevent the terrorist from dying through the application of first aid. The terrorist was dying if not already dead so why prolong the inevitable at further risk to oneself. The patrol had nothing with which to do this and the only morphine ampoules available were individual ones, strictly not to be used on anyone else. His back wound (courtesy of an Apache helicopter) was, simply, untreatable.

Second. Call in a Chinook helicopter with an on board Medical Emergency Response Team. By the time it would have arrived the terrorist, if not dead already, would certainly have died. This would have been an unacceptable risk of an invaluable asset with no likelihood of a positive outcome. One of my nieces was a 'MERT medic' in Helmand and would have been appalled had she been asked to fly into a killing zone to 'rescue' a dead Taliban. I don't suppose the gallant RAF aircrew would have been too chuffed either.

Third. Drag him to safety. Safety from what? It might have been safe for the terrorist in his dying moments, while the team held his hand, but it would still keep Sergeant Blackman's patrol in the general killing zone; an area best left as soon as possible. If that means leaving a dying enemy behind then so be it as the safety of Blackman's men took priority. It was vital to get away from the area as soon as possible to regroup elsewhere so that the enemy could then be engaged on Blackman's own terms.

Fourth. Put the dying terrorist out of his misery quickly so that the patrol could leave the killing zone and continue with meeting the aim: a choice used down the centuries for friend and foe alike with, until now, little or no retribution. How? Three more choices were available to Sergeant Blackman. One. Crack on with the patrol and let the terrorist die in his own time: an inhumane act that would bring opprobrium. Two. Administer an overdose of non-existent morphine: peaceful but with the risk (these days) of a charge of murder. Three. Fire a single 9 mm bullet direct to the heart: instant but with the risk (these days) of a charge of murder.

In other words the choice was obvious and Blackman made the correct moral and military decision if not the correct legal one… or are there any others that I have failed to spot? Sadly, though, it strikes me that Blackman was convicted largely on his own evidence recorded on a 'helmet cam' and yet I firmly believe that the 'patois of an infantry battle', no matter how obtained, should never be produced as evidence in a trial.

Things are said before, during and after a fire fight - for bravado, for effect, for release of tension through black humour, for encouragement - that should be inadmissible as evidence in the calm of a court; particularly so if that conversation can then be used for the very public damnation of the accused by the non-cognoscenti. Blackman's words might have seemed 'chilling' to a Judge Advocate with no infantry battle experience but to those of us who do have such experience they were perfectly normal; indeed, in most respects, rather mild.

Added to that, and against the view of the prosecuting QC at Blackman's court martial, the heat of battle, most emphatically, does not evaporate away the moment the last round has been fired for it is then that the adrenaline, the fear and the nervousness often become far, far more intense… until the enemy is once more engaged and one, again, becomes too occupied to be frightened.

There is perhaps a precedent for the exclusion of such evidence. In the case of Regina versus Litchfield for manslaughter following the defendant's ship hitting rocks off the north coast of Cornwall on the 30th May 1995 with the loss of three lives, the High Court Judge, Mr Justice Butterfield, instructed the jury to disregard any decisions taken by Litchfield after his engines had failed, since these were decisions taken 'in extremis'.

Another thought, relevant to the Blackman case, has to be at what stage, in legal terms, does a fatally wounded, possibly armed or booby-trapped terrorist become a prisoner of war? The answer is 'never' if you are an Apache pilot or a sniper but the niceties are not so clear if you are an infantryman on the ground mopping up after an aerial rocket attack while constantly fearing deadly retaliation.

Finally I do not accept that Sergeant Blackman's action put at risk other coalition personnel, as claimed at his court martial, by lowering himself to the level of the Taliban. He fired one shot: he did not torture, he did not maim, he did not disembowel, he did not behead, he did not dismember and he did not put his handiwork on display. The Taliban's reaction would not have altered one jot as the result of Blackman's actions from that that they were already exercising, and as we expected would happen to us in Dhofar in the 1960s: beheading and dismemberment. It could not have got any worse.

...

Published

26th January 2017

The Times

BATTLEFIELD 'MERCY KILLING'

The legal niceties never entered my head

Former Royal Marines speak out in support of Alexander Blackman by relating how, in the heat of battle, they took the lives of wounded men

[Neal Ascherton, then a national service officer, serving in 42 Commando, Royal Marines in Malaya wrote a letter about shooting a dying enemy with no repercussions.]

The above headline is all that exists of the following article:

My own experience was different from Neal Ascherson's but with one overriding parallel: the end result was similar and one that, I have no doubt, is also covered by the same legal definition as the actions taken both by him and, arguably, by Alexander Blackman - and countless others before and since.

In 1968, across the Dhofar mountains, the Sultan of Oman's Armed Forces (SAF) were losing a desperate struggle against - courtesy of China and South Yemen - a determined, well trained and well-armed insurgency intent on controlling, eventually, the entrance to the Persian Gulf.

I was with a company of the Desert Regiment (on loan from the Northern Frontier Regiment where I was a company commander, seconded for two years from the Royal Marines) when, on the 11th January, we were attacked by the enemy - the *adoo* - in a strength and with a ferocity not previously experienced by SAF.

I was driving a Land Rover with my Arab sergeant major in the passenger seat. Our job was to bring up the rear and collect those soldiers picketing the high ground either side as the company moved forwards in an 'advance to contact' formation.

Suddenly, our leading troops were engaged by machine gun and rifle fire. The sergeant major and I jumped out and raced to the crest of a ridge to assess the situation and offer what immediate mortar fire we could while calling for air support. We, too, then came under sustained and accurate fire from behind. The sergeant major, alongside me and, perhaps ill-advisedly, wearing my Canadian army combat jacket while I was dressed in similar clothes and headdress to our solders, was hit in the right side of his neck. He stumbled to the ground with blood spurting eighteen inches above his head. He might have been hit elsewhere but there was no time to check, nor was there time for lengthy thought. He was conscious and clearly in distress but I had to weigh up the situation in purely military terms. The legal niceties of the situation never entered my head and nor should they have done for the whole company was now under fire: the three rifle platoons, pinned down, needed directions; the mortars had yet to be given their fire orders - in Arabic - and I needed to call for the vital air support if our 150 soldiers were to survive this wholly unexpected onslaught.

Yet I had a mortally injured man to consider while there were others also across the battlefield who, although less seriously wounded, would die if not given first aid. The sergeant major was beyond help but his approach to inevitable death was slow: too slow. He needed pain killers and he needed gentleness. I injected my own phial of morphine into his right thigh then, with no thoughts of murder, manslaughter or 'mercy killing', called for more from the soldiers around me to hasten the process. Hard though it might sound he needed removing from the equation in our time and not in his time in order that I could control my part of the battle and ensure that as many of my men as possible survived.

With the sergeant major's death I was able to meet up with the one other British officer and help the company 'win the day'. In fact the day was not yet won for there were to be a further two infantry fire-fights and more deaths on both sides before the heavily-blooded enemy called it a day at dusk and backed off with their own dead and wounded that, in the end, far outnumbered ours.

It was not until November 2013 and the verdict of Alexander Blackman's court martial that I revisited the events of 11th January 1968 when, for the first time, I analyzed my options. My conclusion was as clear now as it was then. My prime objective had been to fight and destroy the enemy with minimal cost to ourselves, my second aim during those few minutes following the sergeant major being hit, was to make his passing as swift and painless as possible. Because of the pressing need - indeed my duty - to fight the battle I should have left him alone but that would have been inhumane, on the other hand I could not sit back and wait until he was dead. Speed was essential: other, more crucial options were crying for attention.

I have no idea whether my action was murder, manslaughter or a 'mercy killing'. All I knew then and still firmly believe now is that it was swift and peaceful but, above all and of the utmost importance, it was a combination of kindness and sheer common sense. Where is the criminality in that when the legal conflict has been ordained or, as in Dhofar, was supported by the British government?

[The *Times*: An edited version of the above was published, along with Neal Ascherton's piece, on 26th January 2017.]

Neal Ascherson in the Malaya campaign and ES-T in the Dhofar War

…

The Loss of the Brig *Maria Asumpta* and three of her crew on the 30th May 1995

…as a result of which Mark Litchfield was imprisoned for 18 months and appealed this sentence. The appeal failed.

Following the failure of Mark Litchfield's appeal I wrote the following to the Appeal Court:

THE APPEAL COURT
and the Foundering of the
MARIA ASUMPTA

(An assessment of the sailing aspects by Ewen Southby-Tailyour.)

Lord Justice Simon Brown:
"I can't understand - I don't see how we can be expected to."

The Three Appeal Judges in their Summing-up:
"Even at the end of the appeal hearing, we confess to only an imperfect understanding of some of the technical detail."

INTRODUCTION

1. The pamphlet produced by the Friends of the *Maria Asumpta* titled '*To Whom it May Concern*'[8] explains the trial and jury verdict.

2. A separate paper titled '*The Loss of the Maria Asumpta - Fuel Contamination Not the Cause*' - by Captain John Lawson, Royal Navy - is a précis of the views of three experts in ship handling, diesel engines and naval architecture. That paper examines, in brief, the likely and unlikely causes of engine failure and should be read in conjunction with this paper. This paper is, too, a résumé of a longer paper by the same title that covers the most significant sailing aspects of the case as raised in the Court of Appeal by Lord Justice Simon Brown sitting with Mr Justice Rougier and Mr Justice Astill. All the original, detailed technical papers (sailing and mechanical) are available on request.

[8] Not include here as I did not write it - although I had a strong input.

3. The Appeal Court judges introduced or emphasised a number of 'sailing' points that, in their view, helped to confirm Mark Litchfield's supposed guilt. In truth the appeal judges' astounding misapprehensions highlighted not only their absolute ignorance of the status of the *Maria Asumpta* as a motor vessel but of nautical affairs in general. It is clear to me that the judges snatched at these nautical straws in order to give their decision-making some apparent credence: yet nothing that I, nor any of the mariners who have followed this case closely, have seen and heard, indicates guilt to any degree either in the handling of the diesel fuel or the handling of the ship under sail.

4. The case hinged on whether or not contaminated fuel was, knowingly, put into the ship's tanks yet it was argued, quite erroneously (and disingenuously to confuse the jury at the trial) that as a <u>sailing vessel</u> she should not have been in the position in which she found herself shortly before she foundered. This is to ignore a most relevant fact: the *Maria Asumpta* was in every degree a full-powered motor vessel (in the correct, technical, naval architect's meaning of the expression) that went ashore due to an unexplained, sudden, unpredictable, catastrophic, <u>double</u> engine failure. Any references to her as a sailing vessel should have been, and remain, an irrelevance but they have been used as smoke screens by the Appeal Court judges to back up their opinion that Mark Litchfield was guilty of hazarding his ship and thus of manslaughter.

COURT OF APPEAL FINDINGS

5. The following are points relevant to the sailing aspects of the case as presented by the Appeal Court judges and are taken from the Court of Appeal, Criminal Division Draft Judgement R v Litchfield (97/5973/W2).

6. It was the judges' submission - based in part, I believe, on the outrageous and wholly wrong assertions by a discredited sailing witness [name withheld] - that Mark Litchfield should not have planned the course he did because:

- **a**. It was along a dangerous shore.
- **b**. No engines are 'wholly reliable'.
- **c**. He could not sail out of trouble if his engines failed - the 'sail only criteria'.
- **d**. He allowed his ship to become embayed.

e. His ship had 'just the one propeller'.

f. His ship was 'single-skinned'.

g. It was an area notorious for lobster pots and, apparently, loose fishing nets.

h. The planned course itself was dangerous.

7. To which the reasoned responses based on experience and knowledge are:

a. All shores are dangerous. The weather conditions on the day were perfectly acceptable for a motor vessel following the well-used and accepted inshore track.

b. If in a court of law no engine is 'wholly reliable' why do merchant ships not carry back up sails. Using this argument, though, no method of propulsion (including sails and oars) can be 'wholly reliable' - in which case the judges would have us never going to sea at all.

c. The 'sail only criteria' presented by the prosecution witness is an expression known to me solely in relation to sailing ships without engines. Its relevance began to cease at the turn of the century as the majority of sailing vessels were being fitted with auxiliaries. No motor-powered vessel can sail out of trouble if her engines fail but at least Mark Litchfield had that opportunity, although by then it was too late. If the engines had failed a few moments earlier he could have worn ship into Port Quin Bay and if they had failed a few moments later the *Maria Asumpta* would have safely weathered Rumps Point. Nowadays all sailing skippers expect to rely on their engines at some time to get their vessels past a headland, to avoid a lengthy tack offshore or to round a buoy against, say, a foul tide. Additionally, Mark Litchfield was going to have to rely totally on his engines off Padstow - a lee shore - for entering harbour, as do all ships whether motor or sail. The entrance to Padstow is surrounded by rocks and islands: all vessels have to pass close to these regardless of the wind direction.

d. If a study is made of the planned course and the accepted wind direction of 315° T, then far from becoming embayed (the prosecution witness) mischievous contention through his phoney 'sail only' criteria) Mark Litchfield's course was safe for that wind direction, that coastal profile and his ship's tacking angle of 65° to the wind.

e. All merchant cargo ships have only one propeller and most only have one engine powering it yet the *Maria Asumpta* had two engines plus her sails.

f. To imply that, because the *Maria Asumpta* was 'single-skinned', Mark Litchfield had even more of a duty to keep off this 'dangerous' shore is a gross *non-sequitur*. Modern, steel motor vessels tend to be double-bottomed with fuel often carried in the void space but except for those that carry dangerous cargoes, it is not, I think, a legal requirement. 'Single-skinned' is not a known expression - did they actually mean that the *Maria Asumpta* should have a double bottom - unheard of for sailing vessels, motor vessels of a certain age and many small craft such as trawlers and coasters - or do they think that all ships should have, most unusually, a complete double hull. The ambiguity highlights a disturbing lack of knowledge and understanding particularly when produced as a judgement in court.

g. Lobster pots are found well offshore along almost all our coasts and can foul propellers even if they are not propelling the vessel. Perhaps no motor vessel should be allowed along this coast from now onwards. What fishing nets? I have never come across any unattended nets lying in wait to snag a sailing vessel's propeller. A loose net might, but a lobster pot would not, stop a propeller of the size of *Maria Asumpta*'s: anyway, a permanent look-out was kept for these.

h. A number of fishermen, a lighthouse keeper and the lifeboat cox'n said that the course taken was close to the shore but these were opinions from people who did not, at the time, appreciate what was happening on board vis-a-vis the engines failing and the unexpected inshore tidal set. Nobody (except possibly the prosecution witness) has actually said that the planned course was dangerous. In fact the lighthouse keeper's evidence supported the defence case although the judges, because of their admitted lack of understanding, presented it as helping the prosecution's.

8. Importantly, (name removed) was a prosecution witness whose sole evidence as a 'sailing expert' was taken in preference to five others for the defence whose credit was, and remains, impeccable. Yet (the prosecution witness) as captain, once put a sail training ship on a well-marked reef in the West Indies through not using the correct charts. She was only saved by her stout, steel construction and he was dismissed from the post shortly afterwards; facts that were previously unknown to the prosecution (and, earlier, the MAIB) who called him. To my personal knowledge the following was said of (the witness) by the Commanding Officer of a frigate: "*This officer should never be allowed to navigate a ship out of sight of land*."

9. Outside the *Rules of the Road at Sea* there are no regulations that dictate how a sailing vessel should be handled, yet the jury and the Appeal Court judges took only the discredited (the prosecution witness) word as law simply because he had written a book on sailing square-rigged ships.

10. The appeal judges did not accept the view that local prejudice was unhelpful to Mark Litchfield once the case had been moved from Cornwall to Exeter, but this is a nonsense. If it were necessary to move the case at all then the same criteria existed to move it totally outside the West Country's media influence. The same television stations (BBC and ITV - both of which showed dramatic film of the wreck each evening the trial was reported) and the same regional newspapers (the *Western Morning News*, the *Sunday Independent* and the *Evening Herald*) cover all of Devon and Cornwall, so moving the case to Exeter was nonsensical. If the excuse for not moving it further was as stated by the appeal judges ('*To have moved it further would have caused problems with witnesses and a view*') then nobody, and especially Mr Justice Rougier, considered the accused's position vis-a-vis a fair trial - yet the witnesses were not to be inconvenienced (most of whom came from up-country anyway).

SUMMARY

11. The *Maria Asumpta*:

a. Was a fully-powered motor vessel with sails.

b. Had every right to be motoring along the track planned by her master in the prevailing weather conditions, setting sail when the opportunity allowed.

c. Suffered an untabulated inshore tidal set contrary to that hinted at in the Admiralty Sailing Directions

d. Power was lost due to sudden, unexplainable, catastrophic, double engine failure.

12. Mark Litchfield:

a. Was convicted of manslaughter due to the inability of the jury to grasp the technicalities of the evidence.

b. Was condemned daily by adverse comment in the heavily biased, local (manipulated?) television and newspapers available to the jury each evening and morning of the trial.

c. Had the support of the MAIB over the fuel issue.

d. Was made a scapegoat after the lack of any 'Zeebrugge' prosecutions?

13. The Appeal Court judges:

a. On their own admission, did not understand the complexities of the case.

b. Presented spurious 'sailing' reasons why Mark Litchfield was at fault in order to justify their refusal to find a lurking doubt over the jury's decision.

c. Supported (the prosecution witness) flawed evidence in preference to five experienced mariners.

d. Were studiously unable to accept the overwhelming proof that clean fuel was in the ship's tanks and thus could not have been a cause of engine failure.

e. Could not understand that the *Maria Asumpta* was a power-driven vessel.

f. Described Mark Litchfield throughout the hearing as 'this arrogant man' - hardly the words of impartiality.

CONCLUSIONS

14. If acceptance of risk is justification for manslaughter trial every time an unavoidable accident occurs then many professions would collapse. Significantly, in this case no risks were taken other than being at sea in the first place.

15. To avoid being charged after every accident are we now never to sail or motor (with engines that can 'never be wholly reliable') with 'just the one propeller', in a ship without double-bottoms (or double skins?), in coastal waters where we might encounter lobster pots and certainly never in proximity to land at any time in fine weather? As that appears to be the ruling, the maritime community needs to know the precise position.

16. The trial should never have taken place. The jury verdict was perverse and the Appeal Court judges, by their own admission, felt not competent to adjudicate.

17. Mark Litchfield is innocent of all charges and must be exonerated.

Maria Asumpta at anchor off Cowes

...

The Sir Galahad Tragedy in 1982
and Crispin Black's book *Too Thin for a Shroud*

In June 1982 the logistics landing ship *Sir Galahad* was bombed off Fitzroy settlement in the Falkland Islands. Despite being ordered to get ashore immediately two companies of the embarked Welsh Guards remained on board. Here I challenge Guy Sayle of the Welsh Guards for his subsequent libel and Crispin Black, also of the Welsh Guards, for his warped account in *Too Thin for a Shroud.* I was not alone in challenging Black but one of a consortium of Royal Navy, Royal Marines and army officers who sought to have the book withdrawn.

All letters were to the *Daily Telegraph* unless stated otherwise.

Published

2nd April 2022

It saddens me greatly that I have to take issue with two brother officers but well-tabulated history must not be tampered with by forty-year-old hindsight.

Lieutenant-Colonel (then) Rose should not comment on the findings of the Board of Inquiry (at which I was an observer) on the loss of *Sir Galahad* and *Sir Tristram* for he was not in the naval chain of command. Nor was he privy to the decisions that had to be made for the forward deployment of the logistic ships - thanks entirely to the army's 5 Brigade allowing itself to be over-stretched along the south coast. Indeed Rose, himself, was muddling the overall chain of command through the use of his own communications direct to the UK, thus by-passing the senior commanders in the field under whose command he ostensibly was.

Lieutenant Colonel Rickett was not on board *Sir Galahad* on 8th June 1982 and thus has no first-hand knowledge of events that fateful morning.

On my arrival on board I noticed that *Sir Galahad* was not only full of much-needed ammunition (including Rapier air defence missiles) and medical teams but she was carrying two companies of the Welsh Guards. I immediately found two guards officers and offered them and their men a lift ashore - a mere cable away. This was declined as they wanted to go to Bluff Cove: where a 6,000 ton ship drawing 13 feet simply could not sail.

As though that was not a good enough reason they also refused to embark their men in a landing craft half-laden with ammunition. I argued that *Sir Galahad* was laden with considerably more explosives and that I would take them to Bluff Cove that night, after the bulk of the logistics had been offloaded.

I then emphasised the danger both ships were in and suggested the guardsmen must get ashore for their own safety. Then they could either wait till dusk for their nautical lift to Bluff Cove or walk. They refused to move. Astonished at this unprofessional attitude I gave a firm order to disembark but they would not accept such an instruction from a Royal Marines major - then the equivalent rank to an army lieutenant-colonel.

Appalled and disgusted I went ashore to find a more senior army officer while in the meantime the Rapier ammunition and field hospital were disembarked. While I was ashore the Commanding Officer of the 3rd Commando Brigade's Logistic Regiment, army Lieutenant-Colonel Ivar Hellberg, also tried to get the guards officers to see sense but he, too, failed.

Rickett explains that 'problems with the landing craft' were to blame for the guardsmen remaining on board. This is wrong and a lame excuse for his men refusing to get off in the first instance. When they did, at last, decide to go ashore at Fitzroy the landing craft's bow ramp suffered a temporary glitch but this has never effected any off-loading from a logistic ship.

In summary I would like to quote Major-General Julian Thompson: "Amphibious operations are not an activity suitable for part time participants" and therein in lies the fundamental cause of so much that did not go quite according to plan during the Falklands campaign.

...

Crispin Black, then a second-lieutenant in the Welsh Guards, wrote a deeply offensive book about his brief involvement in the Falklands Campaign and despite my (and others more senior than me) attempt to have the book cancelled the publisher, Gibson Square, went ahead - quite disgracefully.

I start with a comprehensive, catch-all, critique of *Too Thin for a Shroud.* A shorter version, that was published in the *Globe & Laurel,* is next below.

A Critique of *Too Thin for a Shroud*
by
Ewen Southby-Tailyour

[OC Task Force Landing Craft Squadron 1982]

It takes a considerable amount of naive-nerve for a Second-Lieutenant to comment adversely on the decisions made by generals and admirals 40 years ago. That, though, is precisely what Crispin Black has done and he has done it in a most unworthy manner. While doing so, and this is odd for a self-confessed intelligence officer, he has come to many false conclusions. In 1982 the author was a very junior officer in the First Battalion of the Welsh Guards, commanded by Lieutenant-Colonel Johnny Rickett, sent to the Falklands in 1982 as part of the British army's 5 Infantry Brigade, commanded by Brigadier Tony Wilson.

For whatever his reasons may be, and they do not appear to be that honourable, Black has opened up many old wounds while fabricating or not understanding much of what went on along the southern flank during the campaign.

Because of the disaster that befell the RFA *Sir Galahad*, with the Welsh Guards embarked, the battalion has, quite rightly, attracted sympathy and has thus, for 40 years, avoided unwarranted focus on the behaviour of some of its men. By opening up a number of old wounds - much against the wishes of his then commanding officer - Black's comments and observations demand a strong repost which will lead to a more candid assessment of his battalion's performance. Sleeping dogs had, quite rightly (and it had been hoped) been left to sleep but now the gloves, most regrettably, must come off.

It's no good Black quoting papers in the National Archives to serve his purpose, for it is the decisions made on the spot, with good intentions and based on the situation at the time, are what count. For him now, 40 years on, to malign through quotes dating from after the conflict Major-General Sir Jeremy Moore and Admiral Sir John Fieldhouse - men of total integrity and strong moral beliefs - along with others who are also deceased, is a disgrace. It is an equal disgrace that not one of the surviving, senior officers involved from the Royal Navy, Royal Marines, Royal Fleet Auxiliary, merchant navy and army was interviewed for this book. Clearly the long-tabulated and well-established facts in numerous unchallenged accounts were not going to help Black's warped agenda.

The tragedy of the Welsh Guards during the Falkland campaign began when they were obliged to be in theatre while very far from being 'battle ready'. This contrasted fundamentally with the three Royal Marines Commandos (40, 42 and 45) and the two Parachute Brigade battalions (2 & 3 Para); also to a lesser degree to the Ghurkha and Scots Guards battalions of the 5 Brigade.

Before I pick through a few of Black's wilder assertions let me lay down a marker: whatever led up to the loss of life on board RFA *Sir Galahad* on the 8th June 1982, in the final analysis there were only two men responsible for the Welsh Guards being on board when the Argentine bombs struck. The Task Force did not 'squander half a battalion' as claimed but Major Sayle, supported by Major Bremner did just that by refusing to disembark until too late. This had nothing to do with Moore or even, at that stage, anything to do with Wilson. Second Lieutenant Black fails to understand this fundamental point. Sayle's decision to remain on board is not once mentioned by Black yet is fundamental to this sad saga.

In two extraordinary paragraphs Black states:

The orthodox view about the Falklands is that all was well from the moment 3 Commando Brigade under Royal Marines Brigadier Julian Thompson had finished coming ashore on Saturday, May 22, 1982, until the Army's 5 Infantry Brigade landed on Tuesday, June 1. It was then that things began to go wrong.

Nothing could be further from the truth. Before 5 Infantry Brigade (2nd Battalion Scots Guards and 1st Battalion Welsh Guards, the Ghurkhas and our artillery regiment) even got there on June 1, the different styles of warfare of the Royal Marines and Royal Navy – and a complicated top command structure without army commanders – had started to cause unforced casualties.

What unforced casualties? There were no casualties at that stage apart from air attack and at the battle for Goose Green neither of which can, in any way, be described as 'unforced'? Additionally Black was too junior to know that with the arrival of the divisional staff was the deputy commander, a senior army officer, Brigadier (later General Sir John) Waters.

Later Black says:

Major General Jeremy Moore took over as Commander Land Forces Falkland Islands when he landed just ahead of the reinforcing 5 Infantry Brigade. Instead of being the solution, he became the source of further unforced errors. Moore was a hero with a Military Cross and bar from Borneo, unusual in those days. But he was a Royal Marine, and the most he had commanded before was 3 Commando Brigade – only one moving part. He was the wrong man to lead a two-brigade operation.

All brigadiers command one brigade until promoted to major general when they are eligible to command a division – of two brigades. This is a gratuitously unpleasant comment.

What was needed was a strong hand to make sure that the two brigade commanders worked well with each other, and that resources were equitably and efficiently distributed between the brigades as laid down in Britain's core military doctrine. Moore simply lacked the requisite qualifications.

What qualifications did Moore lack that an army major general might not have lacked in order to conduct an amphibious operation? In practice Moore was the perfect choice precisely because he was a Royal Marine and thus well versed and experienced in amphibious warfare- including the complexities of an open sea flank, little appreciated by the army - and an understanding of how the Royal Marines and the Royal Navy work in coordination. Black was (and remains) an officer with no experience, or understanding, of amphibious warfare, which the campaign was from the beginning to the end with the naval service supplying continuous logistic support, transport and firepower both from the sea and from the air.

We have become so accustomed to events 'down south' in 1982 as presented to us over the past 40 years by a tide of, at times, boastful accounts that our historical judgment and in some cases common sense have been misled. It is difficult today to make the imaginative leap away from this version of what happened (which out of politeness I will label the 'orthodoxy') and identify what did happen and should have happened:

the war could have been won earlier at less human cost. The *Sir Galahad* tragedy need never have happened.

It is not easy to discern what Black means by this other than to suggest that the *Sir Galahad* tragedy was everybody's fault but that of the Welsh Guards. I certainly take issue with the statement that the war would have been won earlier. The truth is that the final victory was delayed by the antics of 5 Brigade while the Commando Brigade, augmented by two Parachute battalions waited, exasperated in the snow covered, wind-lashed hills.

Black forgets that 5 Brigade came south with neither logistic support or troop-lift helicopters. On the brigade's arrival all logistic assets, designed to support just one brigade - the Commando Brigade - had now to be split in two. Added to which, by his impetuous charge along the south coast Wilson, unknown initially by Moore until help was hastily called for, forced the general and his logisticians into a most unenviable position.

We were less well fed. All the units of 3 Commando Brigade enjoyed Arctic ration packs stuffed with treats, chocolates, cocoa – more than 4,000 calories per man per day. 5 Infantry Brigade had standard NATO ration packs at around 2,500 calories per day.

If he is going to make such petty comments Black should have done better research. For instance, 40 Commando's A Company commander states that they were fed normal rations throughout, 'less one day when some joker gave us arctic rations - devoid of water I asked that we revert back to non-dehydrated food'.

He comments that his battalion was equipped with 'difficult radios' yet later on he admits to using the then current Clansman radio as issued to all ground troops. Black's complaint that his brigade was issued with 'rubbish' kit should best be directed to those in the MoD who sent an unprepared brigade to a war and not those in command 'down south'.

Army troops were to pay the price for Moore's muddled wavering and the ingrained parochialism of those who viewed much of the army as interlopers.

It is unfortunate that Black uses every opportunity to take a dig at the commando brigade in general and at Moore in particular. There was no 'ingrained parochialism'. Indeed the army brigade was welcomed - at first - as it was expected to garrison San Carlos so allowing the commandos and paras to move out of their defensive positions and advance on Goose Green and Stanley. Indeed, Moore purposely chose the army battalions to move along the south coast leaving behind 40 Commando to secure Port San Carlos precisely because he did not want to be seen to favour the Royal Marines. He wore a forage cap and not his green beret for exactly that same reason.

Contrary to Black's insulting comments, if Moore made any mistakes it was, first, to send the Welsh Guards forward instead of 40 Commando and, second, not sacking Wilson. Indeed the army had sent Brigadier Waters south for just that eventuality following the brigade's abysmal performance during its pre-embarkation exercise. Nor did Wilson help his reputation among his team (who openly derided him) by bedding a female, co-opted member of his staff on board RMS *Queen Elizabeth II* during the journey south.

During the initial, overland, move towards Goose Green the inability of the Welsh Guards became apparent as a 40 Commando officer has written:

Having been at San Carlos when 5 Brigade landed and advanced towards Sussex Mountains I witnessed the inability of some of the Welsh soldiers to deal with the harsh conditions. I too had marched over Sussex Mountain some days earlier en route to Goose Green so I am well placed to make such a judgement. The plethora of discarded equipment that we subsequently retrieved was testimony to soldiers incapable of carrying the necessary loads needed to survive in wet, windy and a very cold climate. The Ghurkha Battalion as befits hardened soldiers marched over Sussex Mountain without difficulty.

The same officer continued:

Two days later after the bombing of the LSLs my rifle company came under command of the Welsh Guards only to experience further examples of serious unfitness, of ditching equipment including Milan launchers and missiles, also Browning machine gun ammunition. All of which was picked up by already overladen marines and carried forward. Some Welsh soldiers sat down, confessing that they could not go on until persuaded to do so by Royal Marines corporals. There were confused orders and inept map reading that led two companies of Royal Marines into a known minefield, where two marines each lost a leg. Then there was the inability, within 5 Brigade, to evacuate these casualties so summon a Royal Marines helicopter to get these men swiftly to Ajax Bay field hospital. I do recall reminding the marines of both companies that in spite of such ineptitude the WG were not our enemy. The Argentine troops were.

It is when Black comes to events at Fitzroy and Bluff Cove that he is even more muddled and inaccurate. The distance he quotes for a sea passage from Fitzroy to Bluff Cove is six and a half miles whereas it is, at 14 nautical miles, over twice what he claims. This may be a trite point but it is a further indication of Black's lack of diligent research.

But perhaps Black's most repugnant and incorrect statement, among many, is this:

(That Admiral Fieldhouse's) subsequent secret sentence to the Sea Lords was a fiction is clear. If what he said was true, a famous altercation between Welsh Guards Major Sayle and the commanding officer of the landing craft that met *Sir Galahad* in Fitzroy harbour would never have happened. Sayle's orders to take the Guards and their kit to Bluff Cove that moment would have been the law to everyone present.

What Black glosses over is the fact that Sayle was offered the chance to go ashore to comparative safety until dark by when much of the offloading would have taken place but this he refused to do saying that Bluff Cove was his destination and that that is where he wished to be taken. He was told that he would be taken to Bluff Cove after sunset but in the meantime he was to take his men ashore. Another reason for wanting them off the ship being that they were in the way of the offload. He still refused and his men, and others, were killed. Despite Black placing the blame elsewhere it was as simple as that and had the men not been killed this whole saga would not still be exercising minds such as Black's. The loss of a ship is the risk the navy takes – the loss of such a large number of men is not part of that risk.

Nobody was in doubt that Bluff Cove was the Welsh Guards destination. Moore said so and agreed with Rickett but, and this point seems to have been deliberately or even maliciously overlooked by Black, *Sir Galahad* could never go to Bluff Cove as she was too large. Fitzroy was always to be the intermediary stop.

Fieldhouse's sentence also stood in contradiction to the policy Commodore Clapp had (he said) laid down with General Moore's consent.

"I was not prepared to give tactical control of the landing craft to 5 Infantry Brigade for I was never to trust their command to employ them sensibly."

Clapp was right. The criticisms of Major General Moore and Admiral Fieldhouse are baseless as explained by an admiral who was there:

General Moore gave his Bluff Cove assurances in good faith, probably not appreciating that there was insufficient depth in Bluff Cove for an LSL. The solution, offered vigorously by Ewen Southby-Tailyour was to get the Welsh Guards element ashore at Fitzroy first, and then onwards to Bluff Cove when sufficient LCU lift could be assembled and it was dark.

Admiral Fieldhouse's reference to the 'unusual arrangement' for operational control of the LCU would appear to be a gentle nod to the de-facto (and quite wrong) take-over of six (out of a total of eight) LCUs by elements of 5 Brigade. This 'high jacking' scuppered any chance of the landing craft making the rendezvous with HMS Fearless *in order to bring the whole of the Welsh Guards to Bluff Cove in one lift: and therein lies the cause of so much that happened subsequently. It had nothing to do with either Moore or Fieldhouse despite Black's incorrect reading of comments made long after the incident.*

As one of many excuses for the men remaining on board, Black mentions the well-rehearsed story that loading the Welsh Guards into the one remaining LCU was delayed because the bow ramp could not be lowered. This was not so for loading an LCU from an LSL was always best conducted with the LCU alongside the ship or the stern ramp. A ramp to ramp to ramp transfer in a gusty wind and with a cross current was never the preferred method and could, often, be downright dangerous.

Among other sad indictments of the Welsh Guards a commando brigade staff officer has written: *No ships' captain (RN, RFA or MN) wanted to have anything to do with the Welsh Guards. They stole private kit, they opened, and then scribbled over personal letters belonging to sailors, and they were filthy, unfit, ill-disciplined, unprofessional and appallingly led. In one ship it took the Royal Marines detachment a full three days to clear up after a Welsh Guards company, commanded by Sayle, had been kicked off his ship by the captain. Among other disgusting things marines were obliged to clear up were human faeces blocking the showers.*

The Welsh Guard's performance, when supposedly securing the start line for 42 Commando's night attack on Mt Harriet, was an unprofessional joke with loud laughing and the lighting of cigarettes. The opinion of 40 Commando's Commanding Officer relating to the Welsh Guard's command and leadership when he lent two companies of his commando for the attack on Sapper hill are too unrepeatable even in such a critique.

The only detectible place that Black gets his story anywhere near correct are his comments on Captain Peter Dingemans of HMS *Intrepid* who, fearing a land-based Exocet attack, launched the Scots Guards too early, giving them a 35 miles passage in rising wind and sea against the planned 12 miles (as ordered by Commodore Clapp) which, while considerably shorter, would have been conducted in relatively benign conditions and with less of a navigational challenge.

At one point Black complains:

HMS *Intrepid's* crew stood and watched – a surly bunch.

The Welsh Guards' record for pilfering and scribbling over personal correspondence, as highlight above, had preceded them; it is no wonder that *Intrepid's* ship's company were surly.

At the end of the campaign the Welsh Guard's Regimental Sergeant Major admitted to a Royal Marines general that, *Our officers did not have a good war*! And he was right. As just an example of top-down neglect, Surgeon-Captain Rick Jolly observes (in his *Red and Green Life Machine*) and confirmed by Colonel Ivar Hellberg, then the Commanding Officer of the Commando Logistic Regiment that not one Welsh Guards officer came to the Ajax Bay field hospital, following the *Sir Galahad* strike, to take an interest in the casualties being treated there.

In his book, Black ignores facts and does not interview any living soul. Through a number of red herrings he apportions blame for the loss of his men in *Sir Galahad* to just about everyone else other than those directly responsible. In short this is a reprehensible account and a prime example of how to falsify history.

RFA Sir Galahad bombed off Fitzroy Settlement, 8th June 1982

...

Review of *Too Thin for a Shroud* **Published** in the *Globe & Laurel*

On 8th June 1982, during the Falklands conflict, the Royal Fleet Auxiliary (RFA) *Sir Galahad* was bombed in Port Pleasant by Argentine aircraft with the loss of 48 personnel, including 32 men from the Welsh Guards. Crispin Black was on board and only now has felt the need to put his 'side' of the story.

I have never met Crispin Black but I know and admire a number of Welsh Guards Officers and Warrant Officers who, along with most of their comrades, take a more balanced view than his. They have expressed their misgivings with this book, especially as the author, who has publicly declared his hatred of the Royal Navy in general and the Royal Marines in particular, is hardly the right man to seek the unbiased truth. *Too Thin for a Shroud*, is the bitter result.

Mr Black covers the tragedy in detail before concluding it was everyone's fault but the Welsh Guards. Studying what he erroneously claims are newly released papers in the National Archives (I have had a copy of the Board of Inquiry into the loss of RFA *Sir Galahad* since 1998), the author misinterprets and manipulates well-established facts (getting some significantly wrong), before making the equally remarkable assumption that 'none of the stories over the past forty years are true.' To reinforce his arguments, he targets all branches of the naval service to the point that it is amazing that the largest amphibious operation conducted by any nation since 1945 was such a resounding success.

The heart of the matter has always been two-fold. Why were the Welsh Guards on board *Sir Galahad* and why were they still on board when the bombs struck? First, the landing craft that were due to transport the men to Bluff Cove from HMS *Fearless* had, unknown to anyone else, been redeployed by a 5 Brigade unit. Hence, only half were landed at their destination while the remaining half returned to San Carlos to re-load into *Sir Galahad*. Secondly, had the men disembarked at Bluff Cove, as ordered, the regiment and 5 Brigade would not now be having their shortcomings aired in public.

When accusing everyone else for the tragedy the author 'forgets' that the two company commanders' refusal to disembark promptly, while a landing craft and 'barge' were available, remains inexcusable. Blaming

General Moore and Admiral Fieldhouse is unacceptable, especially as they are deceased. It is an equal disgrace that none of the surviving officers 16 from the naval service was interviewed for this book. Clearly the numerous, unchallenged accounts were not going to help Black's agenda.

Throughout his arguments Black has never understood that *Sir Galahad* could not reach the Guards' ultimate destination. The final miles from the Fitzroy anchorage to Bluff Cove had always to be conducted in smaller, shallow draught craft, in the dark yet the author ignores this fundamental point.

In a series of statements Black claims that not only was Admiral Fieldhouse a liar but General Moore was deemed by the author (a second-lieutenant in 1982) to have been unsuited to command the land forces. In truth Moore was the perfect choice precisely because he was a Royal Marine and thus experienced in amphibious warfare with its complicated command structures coupled with the complexities of an open, sea flank. Moore also understood how the Royal Marines and the Royal Navy work together.

Black is an officer with no understanding of amphibious warfare which the campaign was throughout with the naval service supplying continuous logistic support, transport and firepower both from the sea and air. In spite of Black's protests the Board of Inquiry, on which he relies heavily, established the circumstances surrounding the loss of *Sir Galahad* and was required to do no more. So, why did the army not conduct its own investigation? I suggest this is because much of 5 Brigade's failings need to be shielded from public scrutiny for as long as possible. Publication of the chaos and confusion caused by the precipitate and reckless move forward by this army brigade (central to the whole saga) would be most damaging.

As a postscript to his troubling account, Black states, 'Five senior Royal Marines and Royal Navy officers sought to prevent publication'. He knew at the time that our sole aim was to avoid the reopening of 40-year-old wounds and the inevitable flood of criticisms of his battalion. He also knew that we were supported by his commanding officer and a Field Marshal!

What a pity we all failed.

...

9th December 2022

To Gibson Square Books

We e-spoke earlier about the delay to Crispin Black's book *Too Thin for a Shroud* (TTS) and I see that there is now a further delay. Are the printers really that busy?

I feel, though, that I must warn you in the strongest manner possible that if you publish this book there will be a wave of complaints from those who were 'down south' in 1982 as well as from the media people who accompanied the Task Force. A number of learned military historians will, too, take up the cause.

The problem is that you - Gibson Square Books - have been fundamentally misled by Black. Having read the piece in the *Times* a week or so back and then the long article in that paper's Saturday colour supplement, I was - as I mentioned to you earlier- asked to write a review of the book, once it is published, for the *Western Morning News.*

Writing the first draft was a most disagreeable experience for Black's account is a despicable distortion of the well-established facts. I was personally involved in the events on board *Sir Galahad* on the 8th June 1982 and do not recognise what Black has written. Quite clearly he has written this book in order to divert blame for the tragedy from those who actually (and witnessed by many) caused the deaths of 48 men onto those who had nothing to do with the final events that lead to the disaster. This is an appalling calumny and in doing so he blames a number of long-dead, very senior, officers of lying who cannot now argue their case. For instance, Black's very serious allegation against Admiral Sir John Fieldhouse is founded upon a sentence kindly passing-over a gross element of in-theatre command misappropriation. General Moore went to every possible length to incorporate and support the Army reinforcement elements – a whole brigade arriving without anything like the logistic resources it needed. All this is well documented. Had they been alive it is a certainty that writs for libel would already have been issued.

The most terrible aspect of this book is that after 40 years the bereaved have achieved some form of closure. That will now be destroyed not only by Black's outrageous book but, possibly of more hurt, by the inevitable counter arguments that, for reasons of common decency, have not previously been voiced by those who know the truth…and my review will be one of them. The Welsh Guards commanding officer at the time regrets the publication of this book, as do his senior officers - not one of whom was approached for help or comment. Nor was anyone still alive, and closely involved, asked to contribute to this book written by the most junior officer in the Welsh Guards at the time and thus never in a position to know what was happening. Consequently many of his statements are pure fabrication.

My strongest possible advice is not to publish TTS. If you do, you, and the author, will open not only much adverse comment about the disgraceful and unprofessional (facts currently and thankfully lying dormant) behaviour of the Welsh Guards but will cause immense hurt and renewed grief to the bereaved.

I do hope you will heed my advice.

…

15th May 2012

[I have included this, heavily-edited, letter as it was written to bring to a halt a long period of slander centred around my 'supposed' behaviour on the day that *Sir Galahad* was bombed. I believe that the unpleasantness of Sayle's accusations should be aired.]

Colonel Guy Sayle

You will well remember me as a Royal Marines officer who was closely involved in the Falklands Campaign but especially because of my failed attempt to get you and your men of the Welsh Guards off the RFA *Sir Galahad* on 8th June 1982…

On the 18th April at the Special Forces Club you gave a talk entitled *From Pirbright to Puerto Madryn.* I have been made aware that, during this lecture, you claimed to have no recollection of our conversation on the stern ramp of the RFA *Sir Galahad* on the morning of the 8th June 1982 because, according to you, I was, instead, *drinking port with Captain Robin Green on board Sir Tristram.* This is a contemptible suggestion…

Since the Fitzroy losses were the worst in human (if not in military) terms of the campaign it is vital that the facts are portrayed correctly. Thus you, as the Welsh Guards officer in command of the troops on board *Sir Galahad* at the time, have an absolute duty to relay the facts without fear or favour…

While I cannot comment on your recent - and convenient - loss of memory I can comment on your publically-aired version of events. I am sure I need not remind you that the penalties for making slanderous or libellous comments can be high; bringing with them a further loss of reputation let alone any financial punishment that might be imposed…

…

Amphibious Warfare

Published in the November/December 1993 issue of *Navy International*; an essay lamenting the state of naval ship procurement. **Acknowledged** by the then First Sea Lord as being 'more than helpful'! The photograph of HMS *Albion* is, of course, back-to-front!

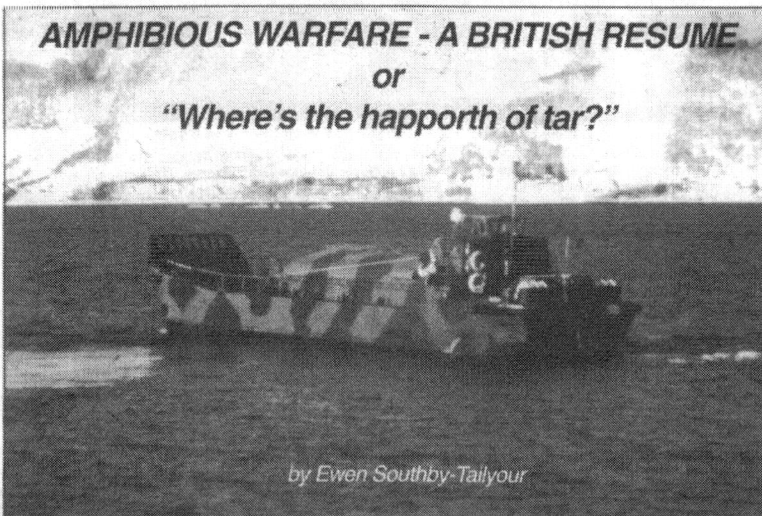

An LCU

At this time of change in British defence policy we should remind ourselves what amphibious warfare, in broad terms, is all about, and what style of amphibious forces the United Kingdom intends deploying in the next century.

No country with responsibilities for the protection of dependencies and trade routes, nor one with a commitment to the preservation of political stability within troubled areas, can ignore the advantages of possessing an up-to-date amphibious capability; nor can any government that possesses cost-effective, dual-roled ships and equipment ignore their value in time of man-made or natural disaster.

An amphibious operation projects power, support or relief, inland from sea, river or lake without, necessarily, the use of formal ports, slipways, Ro-Ro terminals, airfields or even overflying rights. It can be militarily offensive or defensive, or be conducted by search and rescue organisations, customs or drug enforcement or disaster relief agencies, and even by farmers wishing to move cattle from one river bank or island to another during draught or famine.

Amphibious operations are an effective method of deploying balanced forces to prevent a hostile landing, to remove an aggressive force or to support vulnerable neighbours, without the necessity of actually 'doing' anything, unless required or asked. They can offer relief and humanitarian aid when facilities for landing or unloading are unavailable or destroyed. By 'poising' in international waters off a potential trouble spot, amphibious forces provide a calming influence (or a benign but powerful pressure) on potential aggressors without usurping international law nor causing loss of political or diplomatic face - yet they can, when required or if asked, strike swiftly with total surprise and devastating power.

Not only is an amphibious force fully integrated and balanced but it can be deployed from its base to be in readiness elsewhere, without commitment (indeed often without anyone knowing that it has deployed); it can land at a time of its own choosing by selecting or altering objectives at the last moment and it can advance or retire without taking or losing ground. Above all, amphibious commanders can be flexible in the size and composition of their responses and their choice of aims, timings and operating areas: an amphibious response to a problem is a graduated response, tailored, instantly, to meet any objective. Surprise, in timings, and choice of landing craft or helicopter beaching and landing sites, is one of the greatest advantages amphibious operations have over fixed-wing or land-based alternatives. Unlike other forms of warfare, or aid distribution (such as those conducted by airborne or landborne forces) amphibious operations can take place, and be supported, at large distances from the home base. UK involvement in the South Atlantic and USMC forces in the Gulf are prime examples.

In addition to any military requirement, it is an accepted fact that amphibious forces are the most effective for offering assistance in times of natural or man-made disaster. They can operate from a base at sea or from makeshift ports, they can operate in shallow or uncharted waters, especially after an earthquake or flood. They can establish, and man, emergency medical centres close-to, or within, a disaster area rather than forcing casualties to be moved before their medical conditions have been stabilised.

Although amphibious forces are, perhaps, costly to train and equip initially, once in being they become more than equal to the sum of their parts in effectiveness, flexibility and speed of response. For instance, and it is not as trite an example as it may first appear, in one simple and cheap ship (equalling the cost of a handful of fighter aircraft) we will have a barracks, an airfield, a supply ship, a command centre, a hospital, an evacuee reception area and, of an importance perhaps underrated these days, a capital ship able to exercise a calming, political influence in an unstable area. With a number of the world's problems now stemming from comparatively small beginnings in unlikely places, gunboat (or now, amphibious) diplomacy, used at an early stage of a crisis may well come back in vogue.

The Amphibious Fleet Composition

In an ideal world the amphibious fleet would consist of an assortment of specialist ships including all, or some, of the following:

- Command ship for C3I.
- Assault ship with embarked landing craft and helicopters.

* Landing ships capable of beaching or landing heavy equipment by Mexeflote.
* Assorted minor landing craft and harbour launches for 'follow-up' port operations.
* Minor landing, raiding, hover and long-range insertion craft able to operate independently in direct support of the ground and special forces.

During a full scale operation this fleet will be enhanced by some or all of the following:

* Aircraft carriers for fixed-wing air defence, fighter ground-attack support, ASW defence and AEW.
* Support and heavy transport ships - probably taken up from trade.
* Replenishment ships -possibly with some taken up from trade.
* MCMVs.
* Frigates and destroyers for surface defence, ASW, air defence and naval gunfire support.
* Submarines for defence, intelligence gathering and advance force and special forces operations.
* Hospital ship.

As an amphibious fleet exists to embark, transport, land, support and withdraw a military force we must take a glance at what constitutes that force. Its size does, though, depend on the composition of the amphibious fleet although, in that same ideal world, the fleet should reflect the size and composition of the military force. This embarked force will contain some or all of the following specialisations and will be headed by headquarters appropriate to the force level:

Infantry; armour; armoured reconnaissance; artillery; combat engineers; special forces; support engineers; port control; medical and nursing; light air support for artillery spotting, communications, recce, small scale raids and anti-tank tasks; intelligence; catering; military police; ordnance; logistic; transport; signals and EW; helicopter operations and support cell with mobile air operations teams for landing zone control; forward air control; naval gunfire support control; air defence.

It is important that the military force is *dedicated* to amphibious operations, for this mode of warfare is complex and requires regular training at every level in procedures, techniques and execution. The military force may be required to live afloat during protracted periods without a degradation in morale, physical fitness or (a vital consideration) sense of purpose - this requires troops well-practiced in the art.

It is equally important that military commanders and their naval counterparts, at all levels, train together regularly. In the United Kingdom, for example, the dedicated military force is supplied by the Royal Marines who are ready, permanently, for seaborne operations (indeed, they are part of the Royal Navy) thus reducing the need for a roulement routine from within the British Army: a system that would require new units to be trained from scratch every few years - a costly and time-consuming alternative allowing for little continuity or build-up of deep experience.

The UKs Commitment to Amphibious Capability

Amphibious warfare, in the United Kingdom, is considered to be at the scholarship level of military operations, with the re-equipping of those forces now being the RNs top priority. It is best, therefore, that when we procure the replacement amphibious fleet the ships come with their complete quota of 'tar' by meeting the military requirement in full.

So, having highlighted the major principles and tasks and identified the ideal forces, and by making the assumption that the United Kingdom is an influential nation with continuing global commitments and influence - in the absence of a defence review telling us otherwise - we must now ask: will Britain's future amphibious ships match up to those expectations and have they been, as they should have been, configured to match the military force they will carry? At the moment, as designed, they do not and will not, and have not, in reality, since HMS *Hermes* was converted to the ASW role from that of 'commando carrier' well before the Falklands War. It is no use deploying the argument that we managed in that conflict with the equipment we had - we did, but at a high cost in time and casualties. Nor is there any value in arguing that the new ships will meet the military's requirements, for they do not, now, match the original, painstakingly considered (and financially approved) specifications. The two ships at the centre of the replacement amphibious fleet will now only meet a hotch-potch of criteria that as been added to and reduced over the last years in an haphazard manner to satisfy the whim of successive ministerial cost reviews.

Ungrateful though it might seem (for some progress is being made) the question is best answered by a chronological analysis of how this situation has been allowed to develop. The route has been a tortuous one, and one from which lessons must be learned prior to 'the next time': but is this not already 'the next time' for did not the RAF suffer similar problems with their procurement of a suitable airborne early warning system. They wanted the American AWACS but were forced to chase spurious savings by having thrust upon them, to begin with, a system that did not meet their needs.

To start from the first of all principles: an amphibious fleet is procured to meet;

* A nation's fiscal, foreign, defence and disaster relief policies.
* The size and composition of the military force to be embarked to satisfy those policies.
* The distances and time scales over which they will need to operate.

.... which is how designs for the present replacement amphibious fleet started: but they are not ending that way.

After the Falklands War the Chiefs of Staff agreed that the United Kingdom should retain an amphibious fleet large enough to lift the fighting elements of a Commando Brigade; the remainder would be deployed in ships taken up from trade - an acceptable and cost effective option practised by a number of sophisticated amphibious forces. The fighting element to be carried in specialist ships was assessed as being: 3,913 troops; 1,262 vehicles; 42 helicopters (24 medium support and 18 light attack); 664 short tons of stores; 16 landing craft; 8 Mexeflotes. The agreed specialist shipping was, therefore, to be: two LPDs, two LPHs, six LSLs.

EWEN SOUTHBY-TAILYOUR is now a private amphibious and marine consultant since retiring a year ago as a Lt-Colonel after 32 years in the Royal Marines. He commanded units within RM Commando Forces and detachments of Royal Marines at sea, and served with the amphibious forces of France, the Netherlands, Norway, Germany, Italy and Denmark.

After earlier years operating landing and raiding craft from the Arctic to the Carribean and Hong Kong, the last decade of his colourful career was spent restructuring this aspect of the Corps and rewriting the concept of its amphibious operations for the next 20 years. Following his role as navigational and amphibious adviser to 3 Cdo Bde RM in the Falklands, his final appointment in the Corps was adviser to the Commandant General on designs for the replacement LPD and LPH, and for the next generation of small craft. His recent book about the Falklands War, '*Reasons in Writing*', will be reviewed in our next issue.

The Chiefs of Staff statement was reinforced by the Secretary of State for Defence's announcement on December 9, 1986 that: *'Her Majesty's Government has decided to retain an amphibious capability in the longer term ... and we look forward to rebuilding or extending the life of the present ships.'*

It is tempting to add here that we now know what was meant by the phrase 'in the longer term' for it has become clear that Her Majesty's Treasury have very different ideas about the proposed time scales.

In late 1984, a MoD Design and Coordination Group (DCG) was established under DGFMP(N) with the aim of evaluating, inter alia, costings, timings and resources. To help the DCG look at the total amphibious requirements, industry's views were sought (and enthusiastically given - little knowing, perhaps, the pain it would bring).

Among others, studies and concepts based on differing ship styles were commissioned from **Three Quays** and **YARD** and a special study involving computer simulation of a landing was commissioned from **SD-Scicon**. This last produced the unsurprising conclusion that Ro-Ro LCUs would unload an LPD in a fraction of the time of the present craft - a very costly computer game just to prove correct what the operators had always stated.

The figure accepted in the long term costings for the replacement of the LPDs and LPHs, plus the slipping of the LSL, was £550m, although the commercial cost was estimated to be closer to £720m. This figure did not include an estimated £45m for a new LSL to replace Sir Lancelot then on the disposal list. To ensure that the whole project was not cancelled by the Treasury, the view within the MoD was that: *'We should go flat out for one new LPD and one new LPH and allow the arguments for two second of class ships to follow when appropriate.'*

Beaching an LSL, a rare event today. If this was done more often we would be spared too many mexeflote movements and save masses of time

Prevarication over the LPDs

To save money and close the gap between these two amounts (and to keep the vital second LPD) the possibility of extending the lives of the existing LPDs was considered, for which study **Swan Hunter Shipbuilders** was awarded a contract. The LPD hulls were just sound enough to warrant this (despite the fact that the hull is the least expensive item to be replaced) while the engineering and weapons department were less so. Swan Hunter produced two alternatives for the LPD - 'basic' and 'enhanced'. In simple terms the 'basic' was to be little more than a major refit whereas the 'enhanced' option required the ship to be stripped to her double bottom and rebuilt. Costings were estimated to be about £45m for the 'basic' and £196m for the 'enhanced' - and yet neither option would be able to operate the proposed new LCU that would come with the replacement LPD. While these were realistic figures, the savings for ships that would only have their lives extended by 10 and 20 years respectively were not impressive - especially when, due to the inevitable delays all this was causing, HMS *Fearless* had to undergo a major refit that was to cost the best part of £100m. (The fact that this exercise, which produced little in the way of 'enhancements' and no substantial 'life extension', was undertaken by a naval dockyard and not at Swan Hunter did not go unremarked.)

If the life-extension programme was to be part of the 'deal' it would only affect one ship and be an interim solution while one new ship was built. The fact that many systems (the LCUs being a case in point) would be incompatible between the two ships was ignored by MoD(PE) and yet was a continual worry to the users who, all along, saw the military and financial sense in building two new ships. In the meantime, contracts for replacement LPD feasibility studies were awarded with £6m to be divided between the three winning consortia.

The winners were Swan Hunter Shipbuilders with **Ferranti** (and **Fairey Brooke Marine** to build the LCUs), **VSEL**, with **CAP Scientific** and YARD, and **Scott Lithgow** with **BAe Naval and Electronic Systems** and Three Quays Marine Services - thus MoD(PE) were presented with five designs for assessment and comparison between September 1988 and mid-1990.

The programme, which was then accepted as a real possibility was:

* September 1988 - Consortia present their proposals (plus the life-extension options) to the Ministry.
* September 1989 - MoD(PE) assessments completed.
* April 1990 - Completion of final endorsements.
* Mid-1990 - contract awarded.
* Mid-1990s - in service date for LPD 01 with a life expectancy of 30 years.

In round terms the proposals all met the Procurement Specification (PS) for the new LPD and within about £10m either way, were costed around £240m for first of class. The differences between the consortia were minimal: displacement producing the greatest variety - between 17,700 tons and 20,800; the range was 8,000 miles at 15kts with a top speed of 20kts and a low speed 'loitering' capability. The PS required the ship to be built with five Ro-Ro LCUs (one for spare and training as had been the case with the present LPDs); have accommodation for 782 all up (crew plus embarked force); carry 60 tons of war maintenance reserve; ship two Mexeflotes and an American hovercraft - LCAC (in place of two LCUs if required); carry 65 high vehicles (HVEs) and 80 low vehicles (LVEs); operate helicopters from three flight deck spots (and a shelter) and be fitted with numerous HF antennae.

One significant size-driver was the width of the Army's proposed 8-ton, load-carrying, wheeled vehicle, for this decided the width of the LCUs (each was to carry four 8-tonners or one main battle tank) which, in turn, decided the width of the dock and thus the width (and length) of the ship. The large number of HF antennae ensured a certain superstructure/funnel/mast configuration. In addition each ship would be required to pass through the two major canals of the world and fit beneath the Tjelsund Bridge in north Norway. The figures required by the PS were the result of months of careful consideration by the Royal Marines' and naval staffs, led by DOR(Sea). They were not, as seemed to be assumed by some in MoD(PE) when asked later to reduce them, figures plucked from flights of military fancy!

In early 1990 'the rules' changed dramatically and although the reasons behind the changes were based on common sense (and were most welcome) this was to be the start of a long string of delays to the procurement programme, from which we are still suffering. The argument that the mix of an old ship, with its life extended, operating alongside a ship designed for the 21st century would be unworkable, was agreed: two new ships being the only acceptable solution. However, the original sum of £340m for the new ship plus the ship life extension programme was not to be increased and so savings of £40m had to be identified for the first of class. (This figure did not include the 'addback' of £39m to cover the cost of GOALKEEPER, the eventual choice for a hardkill defence system). The original upper price guide for the first of class had been £200m, which had already been seen to be an unachievable target if the ship was to meet its PS: yet the price guide for the first ship was now reduced to £180m. A dramatic reduction in capability was inevitable and the procurement process, based on the feasibility study, was cancelled. The three consortia, amazingly, were never told, each one being left to think it was still 'in with a chance'.

HMS Albion *in the days when the Royal Navy had helicopter carriers. A whole Commando Group of approximately 990 men was able to land ashore from 20 helicopters*

At this time a private study was conducted into the possibility of removing the C3I requirement from a ship designed to approach the assault beaches in order to land heavy armour (always an anomaly peculiar to the British amphibious fleet since the demise of the highly effective HMS *Meon* - the amphibious warfare HQ ship of the '50s and '60s). £40m was all that was needed to convert a guided missile destroyer (DLG) into an amphibious command ship, thus paving the way for the LPD to be designed purely to carry men and equipment - at a saving of more than £40m; but as there were arguments that the DLG would be underemployed outside amphibious operations (there were equally strong counter arguments) the idea was not, sadly, progressed further.

An LCVP

The decision on where these cuts were to be made was taken at junior level within the Directorate of Surface Ships/Amphibious Group (DGSS/AG) and were conducted without too much consideration, initially, of the military's wishes - causing some anguish within the MoD. Examples were: a 21% reduction in displacement, a 60% reduction in LCUs to come with the first ship, the balance being made up of old craft - some already over 25 years old, which would cause a nightmare of planning using differing operational criteria; a 7% reduction in accommodation; a 50% reduction in war maintenance reserve; a 100% reduction in Mexeflotes and LCAC-carrying ability; a 20% reduction in HVEs and a 40% reduction in LVEs; a 33% reduction in helicopter spots and a 17% reduction in HF communications (which were never going to be enough anyway). The medical complex was to be downgraded to the point where, as a ship at the hub of military operations ashore, it would barely be able to cope with its own expected customers. The need for the ship to be degaussed was removed despite obvious opposition from the naval staff - and the likely 'passengers'! The increased C3 complex, thankfully, remained largely untouched but, all-in-all, the new ship would be, in some cases, less effective than the ship it was to replace.

This new study instantly put the likely in-service date back by at least two years. A report addressed to the Royal Marines Chief of Staff, by the Royal Marines officer with DGSS/AG at Bath stated: *'If this new strategy is to be followed it will be seen that the two year delay will involve running-on ships that are expensive in manpower and money. It will mean that we write off the money already spent on the previous studies and we will be faced with the added burden of two extra years of inflation and increasing material costs. Added to that the original design teams will have moved on, which is a waste of talent. We will swallow up the £40m we are trying to save - and more. The ship will be late, more expensive and will not meet our specification. This last aspect is a false economy for in a ship of this size, steel costs are about 2% of the whole. By removing the capability to fill up void space later, any tiny saving in steel will be seen to have been very short-sighted - seldom has the 'happorth of tar' syndrome been more relevant.'* (That was written in 1990; three years later the delays continue with still no firm date for an Invitation To Tender (ITT), let alone an order.)

An additional fact (one that was to be just as relevant to the LPH when it came to that ship's turn for emasculation) was raised: the subject of habitability for the embarked military force. With the smaller (but more expensive - in real terms) ship, all recreational space was cut for it had been generally assumed that, as in the recent past, deployments would continue to be of short duration. The Royal Marines argued, but failed to convince, that future deployments post-Cold War would now be lengthy and far ranging and that the Commando Brigade would no longer just embark for a few weeks each autumn and winter in local waters and north Norway. It was vital that, regardless of other considerations, the comfort of the embarked force was given a high priority - indeed any priority would have been welcome.

The LPD story does not end there. After financial approval on March 4, 1991 an ITT was issued for a Project Definition study, with tenders due by early July. A proviso stated that any company tendering would be excluded from the final design and build stage so that the PD contractor could assist MoD(PE) with assessments. This successfully prevented any specialist ship designer/builder from tendering and contravened the 'whole-ship' procurement strategy (discussed in a little more detail below). Quite why the PS could not be written (without cost) by DGSS/AG, assisted by DOR(Sea) and 'user-input', (as was to be the case with the LPH) remained a mystery.

The aim, then, was to order the first ship in June 1994 with an operational date of October 1998. The cost for the LPD study and the preparation of the PS (awarded to **BAeSEMA**) and for a combat modelling study (awarded to VSEL) was assessed at £8.6m (1991 prices). But by the end of 1992 there was such an overspend on the PD study that VSELs contract had to be terminated. In the meantime, to save yet more money, the specification was reduced further and, with more reassessments ordered, further delays to an order date became inevitable. A date of 1995 was now being discussed, making any realistic chance of a new LPD being in-service before 2002 very slim. Apart from the usual financial penalties of inflation and loss of talent (to say nothing of even more reductions in capabilities) this will ensure that the only current LPD ever likely to be in commission until then (HMS *Fearless*) will need at least two more £100m refits - and while these are in progress the United Kingdom will be without any amphibious capability whatsoever apart from the LSLs (and the LPH if, and when, we actually see her) and the occasional use of a CVS (if they can be spared due to new operational commitments). (HMS *Intrepid* is unlikely to steam again as she was, at one stage, deemed 'so far gone' that the probability of having her 'seaworthiness certificate' removed was a real concern - and that was before she entered her present (and permanent?) lay-up.)

The mexeflote, a vital piece of equipment which has been removed from the replacement LPD due to financial cuts

From the beginning of the replacement amphibious ships programme the procurement route was based on the 'whole-ship design and build' principle, and yet when it actually came to the point the procurement routes for the LPD and the LPH differed so much that confusion reigned, even within MoD(PE). There was a strong argument at MoD(PE) Bath (with which many in the MoD agreed) that although the 'whole-ship' concept might be acceptable for a lengthy run of fast frigates it was less appropriate for a one-off ship. Both the LPD and the LPH (and we have never designed an LPH from scratch before) rely very heavily indeed on 'user-input' at every level - and as only one, or at the most two, of each class is likely to be built these are ships that have to be right first time. There will be no follow-on ships to accept alterations as experience is gained and, as things are, there will be no space into which improvements can be retrofitted, into the ones we do get.

1983 DEFENCE WHITE PAPER

The 1983 Defence White Paper stated: 'We remain committed to the maintenance of strong and flexible naval forces equipped with modern weapons, sensors and aircraft capable of playing a major part in NATOs maritime defence effort in the Eastern Atlantic and Channel, and of deploying world-wide in support of our interests and those of our allies outside the Alliance area. These forces include the Royal Marines, whose special expertise and versatility make them particularly valuable for tasks both within and beyond the NATO area.'

LPH Time Slippages and Designed-in Overcrowding

At first sight the LPH (known in its early days as an Aviation Support Ship and by the unfortunate, but perhaps purposefully-chosen, acronym - ASS) got off to a better start. She was designed (again after months of careful argument had produced the exact balance of men and equipment) to embark a commando group of 803 men with its supporting light and medium helicopters for 45 days - before replenishment.

The LPHs gestation is longer than supposed for its was in 1982 that the container ship MV *Contender Bazant* had been requisitioned by the Royal Navy as an aircraft ferry. So successful was she that she was purchased and converted into the Air Training Ship (ATS) RFA *Ardent*. This spawned the idea of purchasing her sister ship and converting her as a replacement for HMS *Hermes*. The naval architects **Hart Fenton** joined **British Aerospace** to present to the MoD (in July 1985) their design for an ASS based on this conversion. It was an impressive and forward-looking performance, especially as the price was just £85m. There were, naturally, a few disadvantages to this scheme: the lack of a second hull able to assist in the launch of the 'simultaneous 2-company lift' - the accepted minimum force for the first wave of any amphibious assault - was one; the noise and lack of at least a third watertight division being two more. Nevertheless the idea had been born.

In mid-1986, industry was invited to the MoD for a presentation on a replacement LPH. Prospective consortia were asked to declare an interest by July 22, with ITTs being sent in September 1988 and responses due by July 1989. An order would be placed in 1990 with an in-service date of 1993. Various mandatory and desirable aspects were highlighted: she would have a top speed of 18kts with a range, at 15kts, of 8,000nm; it was expected that she would be about 20,000 tons and be in the order of 170m long. She would carry 12 medium support helicopters (expected to be the Merlin EH 101) plus six light attack helicopters and operate these from a 6-spot flight deck with two lifts. She would carry four LCVPs and have a bow, or quarter, ramp.

The final statement made by the presenting Admiral was '*She will cost no more than*', there was a long pause, '*£105m.*' Industry, who up to that moment had been fascinated by this exciting challenge, were now visibly appalled. This was not a possibility. It was openly expressed afterwards that their collective ability and time was being treated with disdain. It was certainly mooted that, had it not been for the slight chance that there would be some maverick willing to offer a solution at a loss, industry, as a whole, should lobby the MoD against the futility of wasting their own money on chasing such an unattainable goal.

Despite the above, three consortia were invited to submit proposals (at their own expense) for the ship. The results produced a varied interpretation of the requirement.

Ferranti and Swan Hunter submitted three options. In simple terms, one met the specifications but not the price, one met the price but not the specification and the third was a conversion of the *Contender Argent* which they would have to buy-in at a cost. A comprehensive list of costed mix-and-match additions to meet the specification was attached to each proposal.

VSEL offered a design alteration of a Finnish barge carrier. The original ship was built on the semi-submersible, heavy-lift ship principle which had many attractions to the point where it was suggested by the Royal Marines (but very firmly squashed by MoD(PE)!) that the dock facilities be kept. The accommodation and superstructure were right forward and, while it met the price and specification, the embarked force would find it untenable for any length of time.

Racal and **Sea Containers** also suggested converting the *Contender Argent* (which Sea Containers owned anyway).

A sharp lesson was learned by MoD(PE), if they had not known it before: if you do not pay industry you are unlikely to get the detailed answers you seek, but the main thing to come out of the exercise was that no ship could be built for that price to that specification. So, in reverse of the LPD experience, £35m was added to the project in 1990. As a result of this the Chief of Defence Procurement (CDP) decided that a new ITT should be presented to industry in order that a fair competition could begin again at the new price, he also believed that competition should be extended world-wide: the then Secretary of State wished the competition to remain within the United Kingdom while the Treasury wanted to follow CDPs line. In the end, though, no objection was raised to the Secretary of State's view. Luckily the MoD(PE) was able to argue that the UK could produce two satisfactory competitors, this point being put to Ministers to forestall any political reason for going abroad. As the original tender had probably cost the consortia upwards of £3m each it was felt that the MoD should fund any future competition to ensure that the results were more thorough.

By early 1991 a new staff requirement was written without the need (it was hoped) of having to return through the gauntlet of further Treasury approval. *'Options for Change'* was now imposing its own delays on the project causing the programme to slip and slip (without explanation), mostly due to prevarication at Ministerial level. The latest estimate, then, had an order being placed in December 1992 - aiming for an in-service date of June 1997.

Despite the 'extra' money being available, the new specification reduced the embarked force numbers (the whole reason for the ship in the first place) from 803 to a mere 500. The balance would either have to embark as 'overload' (an expression which, to the MoD(PE), is just an expression but which to the unfortunate Royal Marine is a very uncomfortable existence). No Commanding Officer will ever sail without a balanced force and all will demand that the 'missing' 300 men be embarked. Men, per se, can live at 'overload' on camp-beds in passages and hangars but their weapons, food, hygiene arrangements and stores all need space and facilities, designed-in from the very beginning. (If you don't design-in these things then a ship, and not just the 'extra' men, really does have problems). Thus very little savings would be achieved by putting the men on camp-beds.

Three hundred men, by coincidence, represents an LSL-load and yet the sixth (replacement) LSL is not on the horizon. What we are in danger of achieving will be bad for our troops and yet the extra cost, as has been pointed out, would represent a tiny fraction of the whole. If a 300-man overload is to be accepted as the norm (as indicated in the new PS) that is one thing but the facilities have to be built at the start - not to do so will severely test the habitability of the ship and, anyway, is hardly the way to treat our men in the 21st century. We saw in the Falklands War what overload conditions do to men before they face the harsh physical conditions of an assault landing and lengthy campaign.

At one of the stages when the size was being cut to save money, the Royal Marines held out strongly for a 6-spot ship for the helicopters (a 4-spot or even 2-, 3-spot ships had been suggested) for the simple reason that if the ship had to be 'that long' it would ipso facto have enough room for the 803 men - even if space had to be left empty until money could be found to fill it. A deep concern exercised by the MoD at this time centred round the view that if we did not accept the ship fitted for just 500 men (indeed any ship) we might be in danger of losing the whole project - it was best to accept what was offered and live with the shortfall. However, this was in innocence of what was to appear in the PS which, when written, allowed for a reduction in cost as the result of 'losing' the 300 but which, in practice, ordered that 'overload' for 300 camp-beds be introduced. To actually design-in discomfort and overcrowding is a very poor show indeed and is not the way to treat the embarked force (nor the habitability of the whole ship) and smacks of a financially-driven, sharp practice.

The author, with Robin Knox-Johnson, the international yachtsman and Reserve naval officer, puzzling over an offload problem

As is now well-known, the tender for a design and build contract was won by VSEL in 1993 with the result that the future of Swan Hunter was placed in jeopardy. What is especially sad is that, despite the Government's declaration that all ship contracts were to be conducted by competitive tender, there is now only one United Kingdom shipbuilder able (or that is acceptable to HMG) to build ships of this size. Despite VSELs very high standards this is not good. What may not be known is that in 1991 a MoD(PE) assessment estimated that there were, then, only two companies capable of designing and building such a large ship - VSEL and Swan Hunter. **Yarrows** were not able to do so without investment to bring their facilities up to the required size. **Harland and Wolff** were not considered suitable from the management aspect and **Cammel Lairds**' future was believed to be so uncertain that they were not considered anyway - and **Devonport Management Ltd** (who could build, but not design, on their own) were not interested.

However, the 'upside is is that we are still in business and in the end we will have our amphibious fleet; for which the Royal Navy and the Royal Marines are more than grateful. But this fact must not be allowed to cloud the truth: for the next 30 years we will be sending our men (and now women) to sea in ships that have not been built to meet the original, and deeply considered, military specification; and for what purpose do we give ourselves that long-term headache - short-term financial savings which have already been cancelled out or reversed. We should remind ourselves of the story that on a military parachute opening the first thing the parachutist sees, stitched into the lift-web in front of his face, is the notice: '*This equipment was produced from the cheapest possible tender.*'... but at least it worked - and so will the future amphibious fleet (despite the same initial jolt of mistrust) because one of the enduring features of the British serviceman is his inherent and good humoured tolerance of the inadequacies to which he is so often, and so unnecessarily, exposed.

To hark back to the beginning of this paper, it is not so much that we are deficient of 'a happorth of tar' but very nearly the whole barrel - which, rather obviously brings to mind a more apt parable, that of the loss of a nail leading to the loss of a horse and so on.

On a final and slightly different note, there are two messages which should be glued inside the filo-fax of every staff officer, designer or procurer. The first is: empirical observations must never be replaced by computer predictions programmed by those who have not been to sea. The second is: the well worn adage of 'Keep it simple' must be obeyed.

Both these maxims apply equally as well to large amphibious ships as they do to small raiding craft ... and why is it so necessary to emphasise these two well-established points? One example will suffice. In the early 1980s a signal was received in the Commando Brigade (at that moment exercising north of the Arctic Circle) instantly forbidding the LCUs to carry loads exceeding six tons. These were craft that had regularly shipped - as designed - up to 120 tons for over 20 years, totalling millions of craft hours in all manner of sea conditions. While attempting to assess the safety parameters of the new Ro-Ro LCU Bath computer experts had stated that the old and tireless workhorses of the amphibious fleet would capsize with any larger load. The stability curves being used for these predictions were those for a fast frigate and yet 'they' could not see the nonsense of their calculations nor the farcical implications to the vastly experienced operators of such a ruling. We ignored it anyway!

The Jester Challenge

To end on a happy note I finish with an essay I wrote for *Yachting Monthly* about the Jester Challenge – the one event I am proudest of all to have been associated with.

Published in the UK's *Yachting Monthly* and the USA's *Sailing* magazines:

THE JESTER CHALLENGE
Newport, Rhode Island - Praia de Vitoria,
Terceira, Azores - Baltimore, Ireland
Seamanship without Showmanship

Saturday 3rd June 2006

At 1150 a huge, white cloud of *Johnson's Baby Powder* was shot into the air one mile due west of Plymouth's breakwater light house. The same happened again at 1155.

Then precisely at 12 noon BST an even larger puff of baby powder was exploded across Plymouth Sound as both barrels of a 12 bore shot gun signalled the start of the inaugural *Jester Challenge* to Newport, Rhode Island. Any competitor too close to the committee yacht, *Black Velvet*, my 12 ton gaff cutter, at 'the gun' would smell sweetly way out into the Atlantic.

There was nearly a delay for the skippers of that first *Jester Challenge* in 2006 refused to sail if *Jester*, Blondie Hasler's[9] iconic 25 foot, junk rigged vessel was not with them, yet *Jester* herself was, that morning, still ashore at Alec Blagdon's boat yard. Almost at the last minute she was lowered into the water and swiftly taken in tow towards Cawsand Bay by *Black Velvet* - the committee boat - while her new owner, Trevor Leek, and recent owner, Mike Richey, hastily bent on the 'Chinese' mains'l. It was, as they say, a 'damned close run thing'...but, to the delight and relief of the eleven skippers of the other yachts, every one under 30 feet in length and being sailed single-handedly, *Jester* was present.

---

[9] Lieutenant-Colonel 'Blondie' Hasler, DSO, OBE, Royal Marines, who led Operation Frankton (the Cockleshell Heroes) in canoes against German blockade runners berthed at Bordeaux in December 1942. He also 'invented' the single-handed, trans-Atlantic race – OSTAR - in 1960.

Since that day the *Jester Challenge* has increased in scope and is now held on a yearly basis with the destinations being Newport every four years (JC), the Azores every other four years (JAC) and, in between during the odd years, Baltimore in the Republic of Ireland (JBC). But…what 'forced' this event to take place and why has it become so popular?

To understand that we must go back to the summer of 1960 when Blondie Hasler's 'amazing idea' for a single-handed race across the Atlantic was first sailed by five yachts, four of whom were under 25 feet in overall length: navigation was traditional and self-steering experimental, yet all reached New York in good order. The first and, interestingly, the last time that this was ever to happen. (Thereafter the finish was in Newport, Rhode Island.)

However, so popular was the Observer single-handed trans-Atlantic race, or OSTAR as it became known, that by 1968 Hasler was worried that the race's success *contained the seeds of its own death*, with excessive competitiveness one of the reasons cited. Yachts of 128 and 236 feet overall in 1976 did not help the image. Fearing a demise, he planned a considerably scaled-down Series Two single-handed trans-Atlantic race that, if necessary, would begin in 1980.

Hasler's Series Two never occurred because the Royal Western Yacht Club, equally concerned that the OSTAR was becoming unmanageable through being swamped by professional organisations and exciting if unrealistic designs, wisely hived off this professional element to *Offshore Challenges* and reverted to running a Corinthian event while reducing the lower limit to 27 feet. A size restriction of 30 feet had been introduced earlier, partly for administrative reasons, but primarily because of evolving international stability requirements which, although not banning the smaller vessels, made compliance difficult in formal events. The result, intended or not, excluded seaworthy yachts from a race that had at its very heart the 25 foot *Jester* herself.

This nautical-nannying (emphatically not of the Royal Western Yacht Club's making) was and remains, a nonsense and surprised owners of, for example, Twisters, Folkboats, Contessa 26s, and even the diminutive Corribbee 21's who were, quite suddenly, disenfranchised from most recognised trans-oceanic races. Experienced yachtsman know that there is more to safety at sea than size and the righting moment of a displacement hull for it is also a complicated matrix of human and physical factors. *The only arbiter of safety at sea is the sea itself*, wrote Hasler, and 'not a health and safety-orientated committee with slide-rules and copious regulations'. At that time Hasler believed, rightly as it turned out, that a higher percentage of under 30 footers would reach Newport, compared to a similar number of larger vessels. Thus it is also interesting to note that the only class in the OSTAR 2005 with no retirements was the *Eira* class of the smallest vessels.

Another aspect of concern to the owners of under 30 footers was the entrance fee which, for the OSTAR 2020, stands at a colossal £1,800 pounds: most *Jester* yachts are hardly worth that price and, anyway their skippers would rather spend that sum on their vessels and not into a communal pot which would, in practical and seamanlike terms, not benefit them one jot. If size had not been a limiting factor the entrance fee most certainly was, along with some safety regulations that were quite impractical to implement in such small vessels. The time limit, to be an official finisher, currently at 40 days was, too, unrealistic for those of *Jester's* dimensions.

Thus we see the antecedents that necessitated the 'inventing' of a quirky, eccentric, rather Brutish solution that would allow yachts under 30 feet to compete on friendly terms with no entry fees, no time limit, no inspections and with negligible fuss, just a few guidelines and minimal interference. So was born a nautical challenge like no other; a contest that has at its heart what the *Jester* skippers have nick-named a collection of 'non-rules' yet a challenge that requires plenty of seamanlike decisions from a growing family of participants. Ibelieve that the skippers alone should bear the responsibility for what vessels they sail and what equipment they carry: indeed, whether to sail or not.

But why *Jester*? Following the loss at sea of the original *Jester* during the 1988 OSTAR a collection of friends formed the Jester Trust, of which I was also a member, to build, at our own expense, a facsimile of *Jester*. This would allow Michael Richey, her then owner who had bought the vessel off Hasler, to continue taking part in the OSTARs.

However in 1997, while returning from the previous year's contest, Richey celebrated his 80th birthday and on arrival in the United Kingdom grudgingly conceded that he was now too old for further trans-Atlantic voyages and so *Jester* was put on the market. I knew Trevor Leek from the two-handed Round Britain races and I knew, too, that he had participated in at least one OSTAR. So, with relief that we had found a suitable purchaser, I recommended him to the Jester Trust as the best option: a view reinforced by his declaration that he had no intention of modernizing *Jester* and would leave her precisely as designed by Hasler.

Once Trevor had taken possession it was only right that we should plan a public future for a vessel that had been described by the yacht designer, Angus Primrose, as *the only radical advance in yacht design this century*. Then suddenly the solution was staring Trevor and myself in the face: re-instate Hasler's Series Two and let *Jester* herself lay down a challenge to cross the Atlantic…and so the *Jester Challenge* to Newport was born. It was, emphatically, not a race (for therein lay legal responsibilities for the non-organiser - me) but a simple challenge between amateur skippers in similarly-sized vessels. It would not be a 'tournament' between professional foes but a contest (if one must use the description) between 'family' members.

Having decided to lay down the *Jester Challenge* to all comers I thought it sensible to study and amend Blondie Hasler's original non-rules which, in part, were:

The race will have no sponsor, no organising clubs, no rules, no official acceptance, no prearranged facilities of festivities at either end (I partially ignored that), *no entrance fee, no handicaps, no disqualifications, no race numbers, no official finishing order, no prizes and no official dinner…* (I ignored that, too, on the understanding that such social occasions would help to bring together what I hoped would become a growing *Jester* family.)

Each skipper takes part in the race on his own responsibility as an ordinary seaman making an independent and legal passage. The design, condition, equipment and handling of the boat being entirely his own affair.

No search and rescue operation will be mounted. Any skipper who is unable to remain alive by his own efforts is expected to die with dignity.

And so there we had Hasler's re-constructed prototype although from the beginning I felt that the need for informal festivities at both ends were fitting - and would happen anyway so why not make them part of the fun that would, also, help 'bond' a growing collection of skippers with small vessels and little money.

I felt that to achieve this simplest of aims we did not need committees flying to the destinations, we did not need lavish parties and receptions and we did not need silverware as prizes. In effect, *Jester* skippers compete against themselves and the ocean with all arrivals at a safe haven - even if it is not the 'official destination!' - being regarded as a success.

And so that is what the skippers do and they do it without having the pressure of sponsorship nor the need to massage images and reputations of either themselves or their backers.

With no public glory – and no sponsor – waiting at the finish, the highest standards of care are most likely to be exercised.

To start with I issued the first and last Press Release in order to get a quorum of people interested; after that I hoped any publicity would become self-generating through reputation and word of mouth.

The *Jester Challenge* was, inevitably, not without its critics with accusations in advance, as it were, of needlessly calling on the emergency services. Now, after 14 years, a lifeboat has only once been called out and that not by the skipper but by a third party who had no idea what was going on while the skipper herself was making her way to her chosen destination in perfect safety. One yacht has foundered following a dismasting with the skipper taken off by a passing merchant ship in a text book evolution. There are, sadly, bound to be further incidents but so far common sense and good seamanship have held the day. Compared to other events where keels fall off, crew fall overboard, vessels run onto reefs despite the most modern of navigational systems, we consider our record to be pretty enviable.

Although, like Hasler, we are not against sponsorship *per se* - one case of Plymouth gin is our tally so far! - but with sponsorship comes pressure to succeed and with that pressure can come poor seamanship which is why my unofficial 'tag line' for the *Jester Challenge* is *Seamanship without Showmanship*. Additionally, *Jester Challenge* skippers are likely to own their own vessels and thus will have invested significant, personal savings in them (for some they are also a home) ensuring that, unlike sponsored, almost expendable, professional ocean racing vessels these yachts – precious personal possessions – will be cosseted and nurtured.

The *Jester Challenge* fills a gap and satisfies a desire. The non-committee overseeing the very few non-rules is just one non-organiser – me! No one has a duty of care to the competitors other than the skippers to themselves, their dependents ashore and their fellow seafarers. As the mandatory 'blood chit' I ask all to sign (the only piece of formality) before the start states:

The decision to accept the Jester Challenge is mine alone.

The safety of my yacht and her entire management including design, construction, rigging, sails, gear, engines, rudder and steering gear, insurance, navigation, safety equipment and suitable experience shall be my sole responsibility. I and will also ensure that both myself and my vessel are adequately equipped and prepared to face any conditions that may arise in the course of The Jester Challenge.

Neither I nor my dependants will hold The Jester Challenge co-ordinator or any person associated with The Jester Challenge responsible for any loss, damage, death, personal injury or structural damage howsoever caused to me or by me as a result of my taking part in The Jester Challenge and I accept full duty of care for myself, my dependants and my fellow seafarers during my participation in The Jester Challenge.

Skippers are unlikely to enlist onshore navigational and meteorological help and – in a parody of Blondie's views – we don't expect them to give a fig about level playing fields but we do expect them to behave like gentleman as far as numbers on board and the use of an engine are concerned. They are simply content to reach their destination safely, taking their own finishing times to then compare routes, rigs, equipment, clothing, sleep patterns and diets. *Jester* Skippers help each other as friends, not as adversaries

In the beginning some suggested I insisted on oil lamps, towed logs and sextants and while the *Jester Challenge* is for small vessels (many on very tight budgets) some of whom may well have been built in pre-GPS days, there's nothing Luddite about it. Satellite navigation predominates as well, unsurprisingly, do wind vanes. With no nannying regulations, *Jester Challengers* can carry – or not carry – what safety equipment they like based on personal experience. I rely on the maturity and experience of each skipper to make up his or her own mind on what suits their vessels and their own experience and mentality.

The *Jester Challenge* – a modern experiment in old-fashioned self-reliance, self-sufficiency and personal responsibility – replaces no existing race, is complimentary to the Royal Western Yacht Club's OSTAR and, so far, after 14 years, seems to be attracting the right type of entrant: both skipper and yacht. There is no vetting system other than my own gut feeling and no one knows how that works or how many obviously-unsuitable applicants I have turned away!

That first *Jester Chall*enge to Newport, was marked by the first arrival being a Frenchman, the calm and amusing Eric Andlauer which, considering that the French tend to dominate the OSTAR, would have been much to Hasler's pleasure: a rather satisfying conclusion. At Newport we were introduced to the more-than-hospitable and helpful Newport Yacht Club and the indomitable Norman Bailey who became our unofficial, one-man reception committee: then and now nothing has ever been too much trouble for Norman.

The first arrival in the second *Jester Challenge* was the always-laughing Igor Zaretsky who was to become Russia's Yachtsman of the Year. However, before that we decided to run a *Jester Azores Challenge* to give those who did not wish to go all the way to the Americas the chance to cut their teeth on a long distance voyage but with a destination close enough from which to return to the UK before the hurricane season. Later still Tony Head - an enthusiastic skipper and invaluable helper and mentor - suggested that even the Azores might be too far for those who really were beginners and so suggested we sent them, every odd year, to Baltimore in the Republic of Ireland.

Another *Jester* skipper - and the oldest so far - Roger Fitzgerald based at Pwllheli in north Wales, felt that two starts would make sense for this Challenge: one from Plymouth and one from Wales to avoid the Welsh starters having to sail south to Plymouth before sailing north to Baltimore so he devised a route that was the same distance from Pwllheli to Baltimore as Plymouth to Baltimore. These two routes (with the same starting times) were short enough for newcomers (and old hands who just wanted to keep in on the act) to sail there and back, well within a normal summer holiday period.

The first *Jester Baltimore Challenge* coincided, by happy chance, with Baltimore's Pirate Week so since then we have made sure that the JBC's dates continue to match Baltimore's amusing festivities.

And there we have it. Skippers from eleven nations have taken part with, for instance among this year's potential starters to the Azores, four from France, two from Norway, and one each from Australia, The Netherlands and Germany: not bad for an event that has never been advertised but one that relies purely on word of mouth and reputation. (The lack of a £1,800 entry fee and no regulations probably help!)

A good many *Jester* skippers have gone on to far greater things and while I accept that it is invidious to name a few names out of the many I have to praise Roger Taylor in *Mingming* who has ventured twice in to Arctic waters in his junk-rigged Corribbee only 21 feet in length while Igor Zaretsky, following his success in the 2010 *Jester Challenge* then entered the Golden Globe round the world non-stop, single-handed race. Others, too, have enjoyed a new lease of life!

So, what next? I am taking potential entries as far into the future as people are prepared to commit while we shall carry on much as we have done so far with no half-witted regulations, no financial charges and no unrealistic time limits but with the most amusing, adventurous, friendly and seamanlike skippers one could ever hope to meet.

[I retired from 'organising' the Jester Challenge on my 80th birthday in 2022 leaving it in the more-than- capable hands of a triumvirate of Jester skippers who call themselves The Helm.]

Black Velvet towing Jester to the start of the inaugural Jester Challenge to Newport, Rhode Island in 2006

A Summing Up - of Sorts

Finally, to sum up my involvement with ships here is an excerpt from my Hauldown Report[10] written for the archives of the Royal Yacht Squadron and the Royal Cruising Club:

Through service appointments and creative leave-planning I have been privileged, or lucky enough, to have 'sailed' to the Denmark Straight, Iceland's fiords and the Norwegian Arctic, to Patagonia, the Falkland Islands, South Georgia and to the southern Ocean; from Hong Kong to the West Indies via Bombay, to Oman, Malta, Cyprus, Crete, Sardinia, Corsica, Minorca and to the islands of the Dalmatian and Greek coasts; from the Gulf of Aqaba to the Baltic; from Florida to the Chesapeake river; from North Island, New Zealand and the east coast of Australia to the Maldives; from the Persian Gulf to the Outer Hebrides; from Italy's Lake Garda to the Canadian lakes; from Britain's rivers and canals to those of Germany and northern France: in rowing and racing dinghies, day-boats, square-riggers, out-riggers, catamarans, trimarans, gaff cutters, Bristol Channel pilot cutters, sailing trawlers, 'covert' Norwegian fishing trawlers, Bermudan sloops, ketches, yawls, schooners, naval whalers, admirals' gigs, kayaks and canoes, Arabian dhows, Chinese junks, Cornish 'crabbers', a sand yacht and even (please excuse me) as a deck hand in a 'super yacht' while 'working my passage' from Nassau to Miami. To which list I must add inflatable and rigid raiding craft, assault and mechanised landing craft as well as small, medium and large hovercraft. Nor can I ignore a North Sea oil rig, two trans-Atlantic Cunard ocean-liners, one troopship, a P&O cruise ship, an 'expedition' ship in South Georgia, a 150-ton motor vessel and a cement-built, Colin Archer ketch among the Falkland Islands; a 40-knot, water-skiing boat, a five-knot narrow boat and a 20-knot ex-Royal Navy, 112 ft, Fairmile B Class motor launch, a veteran of the Normandy beaches in 1944. Nor would I ever want to forget a variety of submarines, amphibious assault ships, frigates and aircraft carriers of various nationalities.

---

[10] Report made by an admiral (which I am not) as his pennant is hauled down on leaving his appointment.

Post Script

As a post script I thought it entertaining to reproduce an article from the *Daily Telegraph* of 28th November 2019 by Alex Wallace:

Inside the Telegraph letters page: from pen to print

In July 1855, the first full month of *The Daily Telegraph's* existence, readers wielded their dip-pens to call for a change that would affect their capital city greatly. They took umbrage at the stench from the "refuse of gas-works, of thousands of noisome factories, of chemical and dye works innumerable, the feculence and excrement" which poured into the Thames. What three years later would become the Great Stink, was at this point just poor sanitation and even worse industry practice. Letters written to this newspaper spawned a press campaign which resulted in Lord Palmerston, the prime minister, progressing with plans for Joseph Bazalgette to design an ambitious sewer system which we still use in London to this day.

Readers' contributions are as important to the newspaper now as they were 51,000 issues ago. As Brexit turmoil gripped the nation this summer, the Daily Telegraph letters' bag grew larger by the day: but one of our readers was struggling with something slightly more pressing than the Conservative leadership election. "Sir," wrote Dave Alsop of Gloucestershire, "why can't toothpaste tubes be like tomato purée tubes and stay folded when they are rolled up?"

Well, such an urgent question deserved a quick response. And thanks to the advent of email, John Kelly had his letter published the following day: "Sir, Mr Alsop can solve his toothpaste problem very easily. For years I have used a small bulldog clip to grip the bottom of the tube as toothpaste is depleted. It keeps the folded tube in place and maximises the paste that is extracted."

Combining issues both paltry and paramount for the last 12 years has been Christopher Howse, the newspaper's letters editor, and his small but mighty team. In a corner of the Telegraph's office in central London, sitting between reams of paper, ringing telephones and volumes of hardcover books, Mr Howse rifles through 600 letters every day and selects only a dozen or two to be published.

The End

Printed in Great Britain
by Amazon

53226348R00130